The Behavior and Learning of Animal Babies

The Behavior and Learning of Animal Babies

LORUS J. MILNE *and* MARGERY MILNE

An East Woods Book

The Globe Pequot Press

Chester, Connecticut

Designed by Maryanne DeMarco

Library of Congress Cataloging-in-Publication Data
Milne, Lorus Johnson,
        The Behavior and Learning of Animal Babies/Lorus J. Milne and Margery Milne.—1st ed.
            p. cm.
        Includes index.
        I. Animals—Infancy.   I. Milne, Margery John Greene,
    II. Title.
    QL763.M55 1988
    591.3'9—dc19

                                                                88-381

ISBN 0-87106-614-9
        0-87106-521-5 pbk.

Manufactured in the United States of America
First Edition/First Printing

Praise for

The Behavior and Learning of Animal Babies

"Two of the best nature writers of our time are the husband and wife team of Lorus and Margery Milne. I can't even count the number of their books I have read and the number of times I have used them as references."

—Roger Caras, ABC

Contents

The unifying joy in my life stems from discoveries, both personal and from the observations of others, about the on-going interactions among all kinds of life and from sharing my enthusiasm on these topics with others of all ages. A reverence for life and a delight in learning about plants and animals, I find, open the way to friendly communication with people of all nations, regardless of language, education, or economic status.

LORUS JOHNSON MILNE

Introduction

Our human interest begins with our own beginnings. The future depends on the next generation, making each of us realize how important early development is.

To seek such information, we look toward animal babies of every kind. All babies start out similarly, with changes that evolve along the way separating them. It is natural to seek details in the environment that may be altered to allow any inherited potential for growth to express itself fully.

In every living thing, growth is more than a lasting increase in weight and size. The embryo of an African elephant goes through a stage in which it is the size of a mouse and not very different in body form. It continues to enlarge until, as an adult, it weighs as much as a million mice. The embryo of the African elephant shares many features with us. It gets bigger and changes in body form as it approaches full size. It becomes reasonably independent and becomes a parent as well.

The stages in growth and the speed with which wild baby animals grow up depend, as they do in humans, on inherited patterns of growth and on environment. An ape or a monkey grows much like a human. A fish resembles a human baby only during its early embryonic stages and then develops to become a fish. An insect differs from us almost completely. Differences between our ways and the ways of wild things show how lives are adapted to particular needs.

Animals live shorter lives than humans, and many are smaller in size. They mature in a few weeks or months instead of many years. You can see the changes in their behavior and body growth for comparison with human babies.

Dogs and cats are unalike, yet their styles of growth show amazing similarities. Before being born, the kittens have been developing inside their mothers for sixty-two to sixty-five days, and the puppies from fifty-nine to sixty-three days. The new family in each case may be fewer than three or as many as a dozen. And just as with human babies, no one knows ahead of time how many to expect or what the proportion of the sexes will be.

As the moment of birth approaches, the mother chooses some dark corner or perhaps a closet with a partly closed door where she has special privacy. This refuge in the human world is the nearest approach she can find to the lair or den she would retire to in the wild. Yet the mother cat or dog often trusts people, so she lets them watch her give birth. And, like humans, she appreciates help if she needs it. This can happen when a kitten or pup, like a human baby, is turned the wrong way inside the mother's womb and needs to be turned again to come out headfirst.

At birth, kittens and puppies, like human babies, are helpless. In most cases, they are unable to see and their hearing is feeble, so they nuzzle at one another and at their mother or whoever will love them. By persistence and accident the wild babies find food and quickly learn to return for more. Kittens get an invitation when their mother is ready to nurse them; she purrs vigorously, and they find milk when they come to her vibrating undersides.

That kittens and puppies are born at an earlier stage of development than are human babies seems logical. A few thousand years ago the ancestors of domestic cats and dogs were wild beasts of prey. If a mother had been burdened, as a human mother is, with unborn young, she would have had difficulty catching enough to eat. By bearing her kittens or pups while they were still helpless, she could travel easily from the den to get food for them and for herself.

The same applies to the natural prey of wild cats and dogs, such as mice and rats. A mother mouse or rat would have difficulty escaping from a dog or cat if burdened by unborn young. Young mice and rats are born as soon as possible; indeed, they develop for only three weeks inside their mothers. They are born blind, deaf, hairless, and helpless. Except that they keep themselves warm inside a cozy nest and wriggle, they resemble little pink rubber toys. But they grow about thirty times faster than human babies. In three days their ears open, and they double their weight and grow fur in six days. At two months they are ready to breed. Such short-term studies in behavior and ecology enable us to understand human babies.

Different as the details of growth and behavior are in wild babies and human babies, similarities can be seen, too. Like ourselves, by the time they are born, all other animals are well along in the life patterns that are characteristic of their species.

Once it is born, the animal is influenced by the environment, by mothering and fathering, and by the caretaking of others. The surroundings will affect the way in which the wild baby or human baby will use the inherited guidance that it receives from its parents. Each baby is unique. As we learn how babies survive in the wild, we may learn more about human babies.

We have companions, although nonhuman ones, facing much the same needs as our own and following routes similar to ours into the future. We can discover ourselves in the unending round of growth and adjustment, repair and replacement that involves every atom and each individual. Through them, and maintaining their living character, flows the same energy from the sun. As we enjoy this energy ourselves, we share in the successes and failures of all our companions. For no kind of life has yet found a way to brave the world alone.

1

Mother-Infant Relationships

We members of humankind share many features with monkeys, apes, chimpanzees, and gorillas. All of us, as well as
orangutans, lemurs, marmosets, and baboons, are mammals of
the order Primates. Our most distinctive feature is prolonged
association of infants with their mothers following birth.

To stay close and benefit from its mother's continual care
night and day, each youngster may have to cling to her fur.
Following the most characteristic and universal of mammalian
behaviors, it suckles when hungry, with no immediate necessi-
ty to pick among unfamiliar foods. Its mother's milk meets its
needs completely, at a fairly standard rate of twenty calories
per fluid ounce. Gradually the infant gets opportunities to
learn how to behave, whether to escape discomfort when wet-
ted by a rainstorm, to recognize good places to rest and sleep,
or to avoid detection by predators. As fast as its developing
nervous system allows, it learns to sort out the meaningless
cues from the important ones.

Variations within parental care somehow even out. In remote regions, among uneducated people, for example, children are characteristically hauled about under a blanket on the mother's back or in some type of homemade carrier. Modern fathers and mothers may use a similar manufactured device to keep their child safely within reach while they go shopping or elsewhere on some chore. A backpack is convenient for the parent and also gives the baby opportunities to get around and see the world.

Among primates the details differ. A baboon baby rides on its mother's hip while she walks on the ground on her hind feet plus one forefoot, plucking food for herself with her one free hand. The baby of an African vervet monkey rides head-first under its mother's chest, where she can nurse and tend it easily in a tree or on the soil until her next single young is born.

Many mammals live in groups for reasons that may include practical benefits of protection against predation and better chances of food gathering. The individuals in groups become social and each helps the other, a key area of such help being the rearing of young. Phyllis Lee of the University of Cambridge, England, described the extent to which vervet monkey and elephant mothers might benefit from communal care in the rearing of offspring. The full range of caring activities occurs in only a few species. But there are various aspects of communal activities among 120 species of mammals. Where there is the full range, the animals live in small, stable groups of familiar individuals. The groups are composed of kin of varying degrees of relatedness.

Benefits of Baby-sitting

Related individuals will clearly have a vested genetic interest in ensuring the survival of each other's offspring. Lee indicates that the network of helpers within a group can become quite complex, but this depends on the precise social structure—in terms of numbers of adult males to females. The nature of the social structure will depend on the species involved and the ecological conditions in which its members exist.

Vervet monkeys live in groups made up of females—and their offspring—who were born in that group. They are matrilineal kin groups but differ from elephants because the vervet monkeys include unrelated adult males. The elephant groups do not. Young elephants in the first two years of life have a better chance of surviving if the family group has more than four potential caretakers as opposed to groups with none. When a natural mother moves some distance from her infant, immature females become twice as vigilant for its safety and five times as responsive to any distress signals. Also, infants play mostly with their peers, not their potential protectors.

Infant mortality is also a major factor in the lifetime reproductive success of female vervets, so help given to the mother when her infant is in its vulnerable early months is important. Close kin are especially vigilant when it comes to infants, and the network of interactions is complex, involving mature males. Lee observed that "infants of high-dominance mothers were contacted and cared for more frequently than those of lower dominance." Yet infants born early in the season were the center of a lot of attention, whatever their dominance rank.

Mothers clearly benefit if caretakers improve the chances of survival of their offspring. But immature caretakers benefit, too, by learning parenting techniques. The benefits of communal care may also encourage sociability.

However, communal sociability may be of short duration, as is the case with the Colobus monkey in an African forest. The baby measures about two inches long and weighs a mere four ounces when it is born. Its mother can carry it in her mouth until it grows bigger and older. Then she is likely to let another female act as a baby-sitter, even though this other may desert her charge, letting the screaming youngster find its way back through the trees to its own mother and a meal.

Trust

At first a human baby does not know which of its neighbors are members of its own kind, let alone which could be dangerous.

One way a baby recognizes its parents is by smell. There seems to be mother-child bonding in the human and primate sense of smell. It makes for identification of family members as well. Chemically complex lipids produced by the skin make this possible. Michael Russel, a psychologist at the University of California working on human kin odor, tested infants at regular intervals and found that, by six weeks of age, six of ten infants could distinguish the odor of breast pads formerly worn by their mothers from those of a nursing stranger. Also, six hours after giving birth, thirteen blindfolded mothers who had spent only half an hour with their infants tried to pick them out from two other babies by scent alone. They chose correctly 61 percent of the time.

In one study, sixteen of twenty moms averaging twenty-three hours of exposure to their babies were able to sniff the difference between the clothing of their own child and that of another. Apparently, close biological kin smell more alike than unrelated ones. This may affect social behavior and lead to a better understanding of our sense of smell and the process by which infants form attachments to their mothers.

A mother baboon remains extremely wary of her sisters and brothers if they come close to her newborn, until the youngster is better able to fend for itself. The lemurs of Madagascar, which socialize in groups of fifteen to thirty individuals, are among the few primates able to trust newborn babies to other members of the group. Male lemurs do their best to protect the group and will carry any baby lemur about, fondling it as though enormously interested and reliable. To see a father lemur offering an insect or other favorite food to the infant he is carrying is to esteem his care-giving far above that of most male mammals.

Other devoted fathers have been observed among the South American titis and night monkeys, where males of a troop high in the forest canopy haul young along with them, although the burden slows their progress and reduces their opportunities to eat. The child-free females catch more than their normal share of insects and reach laden fruit trees to feast before the males with young arrive. The females can scamper more swiftly from predators than they could if they had infants in their arms. Since females of these monkey kinds are pregnant or nursing young most of their years, they are extra valuable members of the community, with expensive habits in need of a supportive spouse. That these monkeys have a strong pair bond is shown by the behavior of a male and his mate as night approaches. The two sit side by side and entwine their tails before going to sleep. Rarely are they seen to squabble.

Ever since monkeys were found in tropical parts of America, it has been evident that, unlike the primates of Africa and Asia, many of the New World animals were unique in being able to suspend themselves by the tail—as though this were a fifth hand rather than just a balancing organ. For no obvious reason, the primates of the New World differ greatly, too, in the mating actions of adults. In South and Central America, male monkeys show none of the aggressive, despotic qualities that make sex in Asian and African animals so full of stress. No male seems ready to battle all others over his rights to a particular mate. American monkeys tolerate shouting among juveniles at play but not hand-to-hand fighting and will separate contestants if the competition gets too rough.

Old World macaques, from the largest (the Japanese macaque) to the smallest (the tailless Barbary ape of Gibraltar), differ greatly among themselves in their care of young. Females form the lasting core of any macaque society, but males as well often busy themselves with carrying and grooming the young. If one male with a baby in its grasp meets another male that appears belligerent, he may offer the baby to the competitor as a distraction or a buffer, thereby preventing a fight. Otherwise a battle may take place.

Grooming

Grooming is a social custom basic to monkey behavior. The grooming individual examines the recipient down to the skin between the hairs and removes any external parasites such as lice, mites, and ticks. Each of these trophies is killed with a bite. That many are missed and reproduce may not matter much since the presence of such vermin indicates that their host has an acceptable body temperature—not overly warm with a fever or chilly for any reason. Variations from normal skin temperature trigger an exodus of vermin to some other, healthier site. The spread of bubonic plague is credited to the rapid transfer of fleas from fevered rats to other rats or to man, creating epidemics of the dreaded disease. Sick monkeys may be too unhealthy to be accorded grooming, unwittingly rejected because of possible contagion.

Special treatment of unrelated young has been noticed in primates such as the Hamydryas baboons of northern India, when a new, powerful male takes over a troop consisting of mutually tolerant males, each with two or three mates and their young. The new dominant male destroys the young and replaces them with babies of his own. Corresponding habits have been noted in gelada baboons of Ethiopia, several different kinds of Asiatic langurs, most African guenons, and the black Colobus monkeys of the Guinea forests.

Friendly Faces

Until a newborn opens its eyes in a lighted room, it has no way to learn anything from visual cues. Within minutes after birth, it is alert to its surroundings; then it automatically pays close attention to the person who is caring for it and quickly learns to recognize that person's face. In a few days it recognizes its mother and pays close attention to the features of her face, particularly changes in the shape of her lips and mouth, her nose and eyes. If the baby does not like what it sees, such as a strange face, it usually turns away its gaze or rotates its head to look elsewhere. Upon appearance of its smiling mother, the baby smiles back. This silent communication delights her, and the two recognize that all is well. In a few hours the baby is noticing changes in the eyes and mouth of its protector as expressions it can imitate, frowning when she frowns, smiling in response to her smile. The baby has learned how to induce a smile in its mother when she appears. Without moving a finger it causes something good to happen. Its world is open to investigation. The infant may be limited to its senses of hearing, vision, and touch, plus a rudimentary sense of smell, but these suffice for a while in an environment where everything is new. In some mysterious way the baby learns to survive.

Imitation

Imitation becomes a means of communication. The baby's first smile brings an answering smile from its mother, who is delighted to see this response to her by her child. Long before the infant learns to say "Mama" or "Dada," it uses its smile as a bid for attention.

Seattle psychologist Andrew N. Meltzoff regards the ability of the infant to respond to and imitate a human face as an indication that the child plays an active role from birth onward in structuring its world. Other experimental psychologists fear that they will be misled by an infant's readiness to recognize a face. Within two weeks of birth, they know, significant differences appear in the length of time a baby will stare at circular patterns displayed in pairs. Pale disks with bold, black marks can be used to imitate human features. Patterns of marks that represent the natural arrangement of brows, eyes, nose, and mouth receive much more attention than those in which these details are in meaningless array. Plain disks of gray or any color hold scant interest. This might indicate the beginning of social awareness, which improves rapidly as the child's eyes register finer detail. At one month, a baby needs any feature to be sixty times as coarse as an adult does to distinguish it. By six months, the child is aware of smaller objects and already sees details only five times as coarse as the finest an adult can see.

The readiness of parents to teach is matched by the willingness of the young to imitate. Human parents are often amazed by one example: the readiness of their child to stick out its tongue at them if they do so toward the child. Just a few days after birth, most babies will perform this trick. Some who cannot, because they have a rubber pacifier between their lips, wait until the pacifier is removed and *then* stick out their tongue in a delayed response.

Scientists are in the process of discovering how competent the newborn baby is. Even if taste provides no clues, sounds could be meaningful. A newborn separated from its mother at birth stops crying if a tape recorder plays back the sounds of its mother's heartbeat. This is a sound conducted to the womb, a rhythmic thump to which the unborn baby has become accustomed. It remembers. To be effective, the playback has to be at the right speed—not too fast, as when the mother is agitated about something, or too slow. A whole roomful of babies at the nursery in a hospital can be quieted by the repeated lub-dupp of one mother's recorded heartbeat played over the public-address system. This may explain why a mother who seeks to quiet a crying baby automatically holds it with its ear against her chest, where the sounds from her heart are most audible.

As soon as twenty hours after birth, infants have already learned to distinguish the sound of their own crying from that of others at comparable ages. They cry when they hear another baby of the same age cry, showing that they are already participants in a social community. The crying of an older child or of an infant chimpanzee is ignored. An infant less than a day old can be pacified by a tape recording of its own cries. Somehow it recognizes them and perhaps understands the futility of further sound production if no one has needed the earlier efforts.

Babies a mere five weeks old have noticed the relationship between lip movements of the parent and the sounds they hear. They are natural lip-readers. They also learn the rules of conversational turn-taking and adhere to these with their peers and parents.

Quite early, certainly within the first few years, children become critical, too, about the source of rules they must follow. Parental whim has far less appeal than a nonhuman referee such as a night-light that comes on automatically to signal bedtime, or a mechanical clock that rings when a group children should swap their toys rather than dispute over possession of some favorite item. Outdoor play may cease with scant objection if the deciding factor is the regular turning on of streetlamps, as the signal "It's time to go home."

Learning to Survive

The baby monkey stays close to its mother and learns which foods she eats, even trying samples as soon as it is old enough to be weaned. The transition from mother's milk to available substitutes comes so slowly that the young animal learns also which leaves and fruit to avoid, as though aware the food is poisonous. Our human parents are so careful while weaning us that we seldom appreciate the risks from which they protect us or even that so many plants synthesize poisons or bitter substances, warning animals not to eat them.

Occasionally we have an opportunity to observe plant poisons at work. For example, the common milkweed includes in its milky juice a poison strong enough to kill a full-grown mouse in just a few minutes. This toxic juice fails to harm the caterpillars of the monarch butterfly, which feed exclusively on milkweed leaves or tender stems. The caterpillar even stores much of the poison within its body, thereby becoming unacceptable food to any bird or lizard that eats insects. When the caterpillar sheds its skin to become a chrysalis, it saves the poison as its continuing protector. The adult butterfly that emerges from the chrysalis is still protected with milkweed poison.

If a blue jay that is accustomed to eating other butterflies gets a monarch to eat, it stands on a branch and follows a standard routine as though enjoying separate courses in its meal. First it removes the orange-and-black wings; then it eats the part of the body containing the muscles that move the wings and legs. Dessert is the soft abdomen—which is where the poison is. In just a few minutes, the bluejay feels deathly sick and saves its life by upchucking everything it has eaten recently. But the blue jay remembers that its latest meal, which made it sick, was a butterfly with orange-and-black wings. From then on, the bird refuses to eat any butterfly with these colors. The milkweed poison has educated the bird at the cost of only one butterfly's life, saving from attack other insects with the same appearance.

If you examine milkweed plants carefully, you will find that they provide nourishment to very few kinds of insects: milkweed caterpillars, pink longhorn beetles (whose immature stages tunnel for food in the stems and roots of milkweed), and red milkweed bugs of one particular kind. All stages of the bug can suck out milkweed juice without being poisoned. Thousands of other kinds automatically avoid milkweed and get their energy elsewhere.

A human baby inherits few automatic reactions to foods that might be harmful and instead must depend on its parents until it learns what to eat.

Communication

The great naturalist Charles Darwin recognized that quite different animals employ many similar facial expressions. He wrote an illustrated book on the subject, *The Expression of the Emotions in Man and Animals*, published in 1872. He paid most attention to facial adjustments in dogs, cats, horses, and monkeys, as well as people from various cultures. His chapters have headings for major human emotions: "Suffering and Weeping"; "Low Spirits, Anxiety, Grief, Dejection, Despair"; "Joy, High Spirits, Love, Tender Feelings, Devotion"; "Reflection—Meditation—Ill-temper—Sulkiness—Determination"; "Hatred and Anger."

Darwin also observed the following:

Children at a very early age do not blush; nor do they show those other signs of self-consciousness which generally accompany blushing; and it is one of their chief charms that they think nothing about what others think of them. At this early age they will stare at a stranger with a fixed gaze and unblinking eyes, as on an inanimate object, in a manner which we elders cannot imitate.

He showed great interest in body movements and gestures that accompany facial changes, for the nervous system integrates total behavior both in human individuals and among other animals.

Since Darwin's time, expert observers of infant development have come to doubt that any emotional behavior is present at birth. Crying almost appears to be a reflex rather than an expression of emotion. The responses with which we are born may include *love*, evoked when an infant is gently stroked; *fear*, elicited by loud noise or sudden movements; and *rage*, with flushing of the face, when the child is abruptly blocked from movement. Or the sole reaction may be *excitement*, brought on by a slowly expanding range of stimuli. Anger, disgust, and jealousy seem to be gradual additions. Smiling may be a reflex evident soon after birth, but social smiling in response to a human face or a photo of it develops by two and a half months and reaches its peak of performance sixteen to twenty weeks after birth. Fear may not show until the infant is a month old, and delight at two months. Most fears seem to be learned and go with the culture: being left alone, being nearly struck by falling objects, being left in a dark room, being close to a strange person, seeing a snake nearby, or seeing a large dog, particularly if it barks loudly.

Each young primate learns at an early age how to fit into the society of its elders. Just as a newly hatched bird in the nest listens intently to the sounds its parents make and learns their songs, so, too, a child learns words from his parents until it can duplicate them and communicate. Already, less than three days after being born, a child recognizes its mother's voice and will work to hear a repetition of it—but not that of the voice of some other female. A youngster of five or six years, just starting school, has already spent more than twenty thousand hours learning to interpret by ear the talk of parents and associates. Perhaps ten thousand complex sequences of syllables have become recognizable, related to events in the surroundings. If more than one language is used routinely at home, the number may be higher because each word consists of special sounds in sequence that are characteristic of the language. A young child learns the spoken language (and the proper sequence of words as well as sounds) long before it can read or write. Prolonged inability to use the local language is a

Young American babies five weeks old do their best to learn early as do parrots, but greater success is achieved because they can sum up a new picture of the outside world every tenth of a second in each waking day. (Courtesy of Anne McShane, Barrington, New Hampshire)

major handicap, for it stands in the way of proper response to warning signs, to written directions, and to managing money and equipment. How could you look up a telephone number in the directory if you couldn't read the words?

In comparing the behavior of newborn children with that of nonhuman young, we must never forget that the sounds of animals form a code, often hidden in a wealth of confusing details. Each animal has its own "code book," its own scale of values. In the range of sounds to which it is sensitive, it picks out only those syllables with special meaning. In trying to break the code, we must identify those syllables and discover their significance to the animal itself. Only then will the creature's actually simple language become one that humankind can understand.

Only members of the parrot family and a few other birds seem to develop the skills to imitate our words. Even a bottlenose dolphin, with its relatively gigantic brain, reveals its own limitation in communication mode when it responds to the voice of a familiar trainer. At best it chirps in a recognizable rhythm that could be words if the frequency of the sound waves were pitched much lower.

Far greater success has been achieved with chimpanzees and gorillas. Allegedly, they can learn through instruction how to use sign language or how to use a keyboard to indicate the questions or answers they wish to give. A child rarely requires help from any electrical device as it quickly discovers how to make appropriate responses. Human memory is biased to give closest attention to whatever occurs immediately after some action and to overlook those that follow later. For this reason a child will learn to read faster if seated in front of a computer screen that displays at once whatever buttons on the keyboard are pressed. It's fun, and the pleasure of instant achievement makes the learning experience quick and lasting.

Some tests of perception suggest that the human brain sums up a new picture of the outside world every tenth of a second in each waking day. During that tenth of a second it can appreciate perhaps a thousand bits of information from the sense organs. In seventy years, the brain might store 15,000,000,000 such items—a number a thousand times greater than the total of nerve cells in the body.

Communication serves a wide variety of functions in primates. Most primate species have communication systems that utilize postures, gestures, facial expressions, vocalizations, and pheromones concentrating especially on vision, audition, and olfaction. Most are proficient in both vision and audition, but species differ significantly as to the extent to which each system is used. It varies from intimate behavioral interactions between individuals in maternal-infant behavior,

Only young Amazona parrots and a few other birds develop the skill to imitate our words just as human babies do. (Courtesy of Lorus J. Milne and Margery Milne, Durham, New Hampshire)

grooming, and mating to that of long-distance communication in threats and intergroup spacing.

Several different kinds of monkeys show a special behavior that keeps both parents together and aware of one another for the benefit of their young. Each dawn the parents sing duets in which the male adjusts his song to that of his mate, and she her song in tune with his. Each parent knows that the other is close by and responsive. So long as the female joins her mate in song each day, he remains where he can help in defending their young. This behavior is exclusive to those monkeys that defend a territory and a mate all year, specifically the tarsier of the Philippines, the titi monkeys and the langurs of Madagascar, and the night monkeys of Latin America.

In recent years there has been a remarkable development in communication between humankind and chimpanzees in the laboratory using symbols and American sign language. Individual chimps have learned from one hundred to one thousand signs. They are capable of forming simple sentences and even "conversing" with human experimenters by means of these signs.

Family Structures

One way that primate behavioral development contrasts with that of other mammalian orders is the relatively long period of infant dependency upon the mother. Many species of monkeys are physically weaned at about one year of age, but they retain close relationships with their mothers for two or three years and deferential behavior toward her throughout their lives. It is during this rather long period of infant dependency and social relationship that the behavioral skills of the species and the social traditions of the group are acquired. In some of the lower primates the period of infant dependency may be much shorter—as little as four weeks in tree shrews, for example, but longer in the great apes. In the chimpanzee, suckling and other forms of infant dependency persist for several years, and the weaning process is prolonged, often requiring a span of two or three years. The first signs of maternal rejection at nursing may start when the infant is two years old but may not be complete until it is four or more years of age.

Even young wild primates need to know how their society operates. Gibbons in the East Indies and some of the African apes live in monogamous pairs, one male and one female plus their immediate offspring. Youngsters have to learn which is their family and stay with it. We could wish that gibbons were closer primate kin, for they are the only relatives with good voices, which they raise in chorus from treetops lit by the first rays of dawn. Their societies seem mimicked by the lemurs and indri of Madagascar and by marmosets, titis, and night monkeys of the New World.

Gorillas form little clusters around mature males, which are recognizable as "silverbacks" because their hair color is so unlike that of immature blackbacks. Each silverback, weighing nearly four hundred pounds, shyly defends his territory and, within it, his two-hundred-pound mates and three- to thirty-pound young. Where his boundary comes close to that of another silverback he watches his neighbor carefully, making mock rushing attacks, roaring and beating his chest *pok-pok-pok* as though it were a great drum to warn off a potential trespasser.

Gorillas live in relatively stable, cohesive social units known as groups, whose compositions are altered by births, deaths, and occasional movements of individuals in or out of a group. Group sizes vary from two to twenty animals and average about ten individuals.

The prolonged period of association of the young with their parents, peers, and siblings offers the gorilla a unique and secure type of familial organization bonded by strong kin ties. As the male and female offspring approach sexual maturity, they often leave their natal groups. The dispersal of mating individuals is perhaps an evolved pattern to reduce the effects of inbreeding, though it seems that maturing individuals are more likely to migrate when there are no breeding opportunities within the group into which they are born.

Mother gorillas with young retreat to a safe distance and remain quiet. During an infant's first months, most play activities involve body contact with, or occur within arm's reach of, the mother. Each baby less than four months old clings to its mother's front or, if older, rides on her back until two and a half years old, when it can be weaned and become independent. For the first few weeks of its life, a newborn gorilla's skin is usually pink or tan on its face, palms, and soles; pigment spots may remain on its feet until age two. Thereafter, it develops a distinctive "nose print" as a pattern of lasting wrinkles above its nostrils, by means of which it can be recognized as an individual. Often, the pattern of wrinkles on a young gorilla is so similar to the wrinkles on its mother and father that the family relationship is obvious to an observant person. The youngster will remain with its group at least until maturity, learning from its peers and elders.

Gorillas communicate with each other by warning coughs, gentle belching, calls of contentment, piglike warning grunts, and a host of familiar sounds of scratching, munching wild celery, breaking branches, and climbing rough-barked trees. Imitating older individuals, the young eat wild celery, thistles, nettles, blackberries, bracket fungi, grubs, and worms but not the hard tree bark that appeals to full-grown individuals. Giant oldsters eat almost continuously during the day, having a greater need for food in bulk than youngsters, which take time out for play. They climb, jump off, roll, laugh, get back up, and do it all over again. Wayne McGuire, who associated for five years in Rwanda with the mountain gorillas that had become used to researcher Dian Fossey, found that youngsters would steal film, camera lenses, and other treasures, then carry them off and lose them if he interfered. Ignored, they set the objects down unharmed and found other entertainment. Most taxing were the young males, already well grown, who would grab hold of him and pull. "You just lie back and let him do whatever he wants with you, since he's probably six times as strong as you are." Older animals, still more powerful, have learned from childish play and seem comparatively sedate.

Bushbaby infants adjust to a very different society, with isolated males defending their African territories, which overlap slightly. Within each territory, mated pairs have their own little domains, each a haven for their most recent babies. Only along the shared boundary between two large territories, which are claimed by rival solitary males, do separate females tend their young in the overlapping areas, subject to visits by the dominant male from either side.

Chimpanzees follow a still different system, with clusters of related adult females living close together in one African forest area, at a slight distance from the next cluster of females and having friendly relations with them whenever both travel to the same food-bearing tree and thus come close together. Each female in a cluster has her own small territory in which she looks after the needs of her latest youngster. Males stay just outside each cluster of females and young and seldom interchange with those of an adjacent cluster even though female chimpanzees may switch allegiance whenever clusters approach and socialize.

Orangutans are more solitary, each mother with her baby high in the trees of the rain forest on the island of Borneo or nearby. After it is weaned, a young orangutan no longer shares the treetop nest its mother builds anew each afternoon.

With the orangutan, as with all primates, there is a long period of infant dependency upon the mother. The baby retains a close relationship for two or three years, during which the behavioral skills are acquired. (Courtesy of V. Q. Taylor, Hampton, New Hampshire)

It must provide new nests of its own, of similar design, in which to lie all night long, prevented from falling out by wrapping its fingers and toes around tree branches. Alone for the first time in its life through the dangerous dark hours, it must not whimper or make a move that could reveal its location to some hungry prowler.

It is unfortunate that most of these primate societies live in the wilds of Africa and tropical Asia, where the learning processes of their babies are so difficult to study. When brought into a zoo or a laboratory for observation, their behavior changes because they react to their confinement. We have no way to know whether adult primates, captured in their native haunts and provided in a cage with substitutes for home conditions, miss the sounds and scents to which they were formerly accustomed. The ability to see in adjacent cages some of the creatures they once knew as neighbors may have a quieting, comforting effect. Yet we need to know how eye-minded these particular primates were in the wild. Many move about chiefly at night when senses other than vision must have greater importance.

As we strive to imagine the wild world through the sensory systems of nonhuman life, it is tempting to wonder whether humans or nonhumans are better fitted to react to the world. Suppose we could "swap even." With what other animal would we be willing to trade eyes? Perhaps the horse—able to see well both by day and night—or the lion, or the seal, or the owl? We would have to give up color vision if we exchanged with any of these and would no longer be able to read the fine print at the bottom of a contract. Possibly with the ostrich, or the eagle, or the octopus? All of these have color vision but cannot see well after dark. If we insist on retaining our present advantages—night vision, color vision, and fine resolution by day—about the only candidate for a swap would be the gorilla. Would we be any better off?

Later Child Care

We can only sympathize with the newborn baby Rhesus monkeys from India that Wisconsin psychologist Harry F. Harlow separated from their mothers and caged for two days, providing them with only an imitation parent and food. The substitute mothers were doll-like mannequins, artifically warmed, each with a baby bottle of milk and a single nipple to provide nourishment. The babies rejected those made of bare chicken wire and clung to others of wood coated with terry cloth as imitation fur. They rushed back to "her" when frightened in any way or curled up in a corner of the bare room, covering their eyes and ears with their arms as best they could.

The infants seemed to soak up self-confidence and a sense of security from their cloth-covered surrogate much faster if the "mother" rocked back and forth gently. Yet a real difference remained. No imitation mother lost patience with the baby monkey. Never did "she" cuff it for maltreating "her"—such as trying to unscrew "her" head. All primate young seem to need being tousled somewhat, especially while infants. Anything less than physical damage seems to have the same effect. A father's firm caress engenders as much baby love as a mother's gentle fingers. The touch contacts of rough play seem essential in the development of a normal, friendly personality. A quota of social bumps and bruises, acquired through parental handling and contact with companions, somehow produces a well-adjusted attitude to the world around us.

Play

The playful antics of young animals seem directed toward unconscious achievement of a high standard of physical fitness. The child has time to play and begins almost as soon as it is born. Nature photographer Marty Stouffer suggests that we should find in play a good reason why animals have a childhood. Practice permits them to hone their nervous-muscular responses toward future needs which are geared more obviously to survival.

It is easy to reach such a conclusion from watching newborn pronghorn "antelopes" in the American West. Fawns begin jumping and twisting their bodies into extreme positions as early as two days of age, the intensity of play increasing and duration lengthening to a peak in their third to fourth weeks. Play occurs especially at dawn and dusk, just after the mother has suckled her young. Quickly it turns into high-speed running, which was much more important a few thousand years ago than at present. Pronghorn fawns can now outrun any predator in their community, for the Ice Age cheetah has become extinct and so has a long-legged hyena that must once have been a major hazard.

At least fifty-seven different kinds of cud-chewing mammals, representing every one of the different families, play when young and later find different activities to occupy their time. Play may be essential, too, in establishing a hierarchy of dominance within members of a species. Young ibex kids butt their heads or neck wrestle while learning which is the stronger and more adept. Giraffes continue into adulthood swinging their long necks at one another. Even young hippopotamuses spend hours grappling mouth to mouth in mock biting. These are significant parts of growing up, of establishing a place in a social organization.

Without play the individual may not function well alone. As Dr. Harlow's deprived babies grew older, they showed complete intolerance for other monkeys of their own kind, attacking them or running from them to continue a solitary way of life. Later, when some of these deprived monkeys had babies

Giraffes are cud-chewing mammals and play when young. Play is essential in establishing a hierarchy of dominance within members of a species. It is a part of growing up, as is the transition away from mother's milk.
(Courtesy of Satour, South Africa Tourist Corporation)

of their own, they rejected these babies, with no idea of how to care for them.

Surely a little girl learns from her human mother through play at an early age how to tend the babies she may have eventually. A doll becomes a practice baby toward a time when the girl child grows older. Little boys may enjoy having a teddy bear to hug, but when they have children of their own, they need guidance on how to care for them and additional practice later.

Inborn features of the baby make a difference in its reactions to other babies and to its parents. Harvard University psychologist Jerome Kagan and his colleagues found that approximately 10 percent of children are shy with strangers and extremely cautious in unfamiliar situations. They tend to retain this sign of mental stress as inhibition and to show more dilated pupils as well as faster (and more stable) heart action. They cling to their mothers and develop more allergies than uninhibited, outgoing children. Stephen Suomi, of the National Institutes of Health, recognizes the same features in the development of Rhesus monkeys. Without help, these tensions spill over into later life. As might be predicted, "uptight" monkeys at any age respond favorably to drugs used to treat depression and panic attacks in people. Suomi suspects that a high sensitivity to stress goes with fast metabolism of these drugs. Sensitive, nurturing parenting affords a preferred treatment for shyness and tension. Olive baboons in Kenya may achieve similar avoidance of stress by raising their own status among neighbors through conspicuous threat displays—such as yawning widely to expose their formidable canine teeth.

In caring for babies, many a parent adjusts the nurturing in relation to the sex of the infant. Experiences with others of their social group certainly teach the young what members of their particular sex can expect. Inherited nature and environmental nurture combine for a recognizable outcome. The young learn from their elders how to survive later, when on their own.

2

Earliest Social Life

Must a newborn human baby learn to be more than a social animal? Must it replace a primarily animal nature while joining the human society of its parents? Searching into the social life of other animals reveals much to be discovered. The success of the ancient ant is attributed to the interplay of individuals in the colony. An alert ant is very active while tending eggs or young. Close association with others of its own kind is essential. Individuals cannot survive alone. Their future is predetermined by their inherent patterns of social behavior.

Ants

About six hundred different kinds of ants live in the United States. Each kind chooses a slightly different way of life. Some prefer open grasslands with few trees; others prefer forests with little grass; and a few thrive in deserts.

Common field ants build mounds. On clear days, except in winter, the sun warms the surface of the ant mount. The warmth extends downward an inch or so and spreads quickly

27

because the ants have dug dozens of small chambers, each with an earthen roof barely an eighth of an inch thick. To these chambers the ants bring the eggs that the queen has laid. They hatch sooner with the extra heat. The ants carry the grublike hatchlings to safer depths for the night and then return them to the warm nurseries the next sunny day. This helps the young digest their food faster and grow more quickly.

Eventually, each immature ant spins a cocoon around itself. Inside the cocoon it has the privacy in which to change into an adult ant. This change occurs more rapidly if the queen's daughters carry the cocoons into the warm chambers as often as possible. Each cocoon resembles a soft grain of puffed rice. Its concealed occupant soon cuts its way out and becomes another working ant in the nest.

There is plenty of work to be done underground. Eggs and young must be carried up and down the nest. Food must be received from worker ants that have been foraging outdoors. Particles of earth must be removed to make more storage chambers. If a tunnel collapses, it must be cleared. If an ant dies inside the nest, the body must be dragged outside the doorway and disposed of. And most important, the queen must be cleaned and well fed.

The field-ant colony is composed of different groups of individuals, each with a particular task. Worker ants that venture into the open risk their lives while hunting for food. Their eyes are not nearly as good as those of the wolf spider that watches for an ant to come along.

Ants in temperate lands hurry about in search of food almost exclusively after the sun rises and before it sets. The sun becomes a sort of guiding star which helps the ant find its way home again by a different route. To use the sun in this way requires only mediocre eyesight; a special memory keeps track of every turn and detour. Each ant also provides itself with a second means of getting home in case clouds hide the sun. As it travels, the ant keeps touching the tip of its body against the ground, leaving a chemical trail. If all else fails, the ant can find this trail again. The insect's sensitive feelers tap against the ground and pick up the scent. The ant retraces its steps, even though the route is long and irregular, and eventually arrives home. In many ants, chemoreception is the primary sense.

When an ant goes home with food, usually by the most direct path it can find, it leaves a slightly different trail of odorous materials. These chemical secretions are daubed on the ground at frequent intervals and form a series of trail markers, which other ants from the nest can follow to the food source. A large number of ants may arrive in short order at a picnic table that a single ant has discovered.

Such a trail of ants is just what a flicker likes to find. This large woodpecker settles itself quietly on the ground at one side of the trail and eats each ant as it comes along. Still better for the bird, and worse for the ant, is for the flicker to discover the dome of the nest. The bird uses its beak to open the chambers where the ants are warming their eggs, young, and cocoons. Before the workers can carry their treasures to deeper safety, the flicker gulps down dozens of them.

Any ant risks its life when it goes outside the nest to search for food. Only a few of the many thousands in a colony take this chance at any one time. Most of the ants stay below ground, where the queen, the masses of stored food, and many of the young seem safe. Even those ants that venture outside on sunny days seldom need to hunt for hours to find trophies to carry home. The list of useful, acceptable items is almost endless. A grass seed can be grasped in the ant's jaws and doesn't interfere with running along the trail. A drop of honeydew may be sucked from an aphid that is feeding on a plant. The liquid is rich in sugars and disappears inside the ant as neatly as gasoline into the storage tank of an automobile. A little of the sugar nourishes the ant, providing it with useful energy, while the remainder will be shared with other members of the colony inside the nest.

The ants of America north of Mexico and of temperate parts of Eurasia show far more similarity in their behavior than the nearly three thousand kinds that live in the tropics.

Most famous of the tropical ants are those that follow a gypsy lifestyle, with no permanent home of any kind. Those living in Central and South America are known as *army ants*, while the African ants with similar habits are called *driver ants*. These ants differ in ways that only a scientist is likely to appreciate. All of them move about, taking their queen along.

The queen makes this possible by staying slim enough to travel with her army for about seventeen consecutive nights. After that, the entire colony takes a three-week holiday. The first week the queen rests and grows amazingly plump. During the next week she lays eggs at a frantic pace—as many as a hundred thousand of them. She rests again during the week needed for the eggs to hatch and gets back into shape for further travel. Then off go the ants again, to a new camp-site every night, a new hunting operation every day.

The queen of the army is usually the largest member of the colony. The smallest of her daughters tend to her constantly. Larger daughters, which are nearly twice the size of their smaller sisters and far more numerous, do most of the work. Still larger daughters guard the outer boundaries of the colony. These guards possess enormous heads and hook-shaped jaws so huge that they must rely on smaller workers to feed them. At the slightest commotion, these jaws open wide. The guard bites down hard on any intruder, while stabbing repeatedly with a venomous stinger at the rear of its body.

Before dark each day during the hunting season, all of the ants prepare to move onward. Nearly a hundred thousand of the middle-size workers find a grublike youngster to transport. Each one is picked up gently in tonglike jaws. The ant army then heads to its next destination, carrying the young along, helping the queen with her retinue to keep up.

By midnight the army sometimes finds a stopping place. The ants cluster there until dawn, in a temporary encampment that a military person would call a bivouac. The bivouac is the day's resting place for the queen, her young, her tiny attendant daughters, perhaps a thousand of the middle-sized workers, and a good many guards. The rest of the colony marches off in various directions. Big-headed guards appear at intervals along both sides of the columns, to keep each stream of marchers in a tidy line. Each moving column has no leader to show it the way to go. Like a miniature flood four inches wide, it pours along. The ants at the leading edge seem unwilling to be pushed into unfamiliar territory; they turn and try to get back among the oncoming throng. But advancing ants shove the timid ones aside. The column discovers beetles, grasshoppers, lizards, and nestling birds that have not been able to escape. Promptly the ants overwhelm each prize. They cut it into pieces which they can carry back alongside the line of march.

Although a dead fly, caterpillar, or some other irregular piece of meat is less convenient to transport, several ants can cooperate in hauling such a bulky prize. Or they may use their jaws to cut the meat into pieces, each small enough for an individual ant to manage.

The trophies are moved steadily toward the place where the queen, her brood, and her retinue are waiting. But much of the nourishment is devoured by advancing workers along the way. If the hunting is good, the queen and her growing young get plenty of food from the many columns. The tiny workers take their share as they prepare the food to feed the queen, the immature ants, and the big-headed guards.

The hungry young of the army ants are the ones that keep

the workers busy. The young exude a flavorsome secretion that excites the workers. The adults obtain this exciting substance while transporting the grubs each night. A worker that finds no youngster to carry goes repeatedly to lick one that some other ant is holding. When the young attain full size and spin cocoons around themselves, the workers can no longer obtain the exciting substance during the nightly travel hours. Then the workers seem to go on strike. They laze about all day, neither marching off to hunt for food nor readying themselves for a move to a new site after dark. In the first week the queen grows obese. The next week she lays her eggs. One more week is needed for the eggs to develop and for the young in the cocoons to reach adult form. Then everything happens at once: The new adults emerge from the cocoons, the eggs hatch, releasing thousands of young, and the workers once again taste the substance that urges the army into action. The time of rest and relaxation is over, and the ants begin marching off again, in different patterns by night and by day. Each night their queen is ready to go along, like a gypsy queen with daughters forming her caravan.

Among army ants the queen may live as long as five years. During the last half of her reign she produces some slightly different young. A few mature as virgin queens; like their mother, they lack wings entirely. A hundred or more become winged males and survive only a week or two. The lucky ones fly by night to other colonies that have a virgin queen waiting for a mate. A mated queen can induce some workers to help her found a new colony. Soon she replaces them with working daughters of her own. Her success is limited mostly by the hunting habits of the workers. They expend so much energy in finding and overpowering their prey that only the surplus food can go to the queen and her young. On a poor day the hunting may yield very little, while on a good one it can yield the nourishment from half a million insects, a snake or two, and extra tidbits. All of this contributes to the vigor of the entire army-ant colony.

Leaf-cutter ants seem satisfied with vegetable food. They find what they need with far less effort and store their trophies in cavernous chambers, like cellars, underground. Some even raise fungi, like miniature mushrooms, on compost heaps made of leaf pieces, which their workers have cut and brought to the nest. Usually the colonies are numerous and their exploits much less dramatic than those of army ants. Their queens produce a new brood of winged females and winged males at least once each year. They are stick-at-homes instead of gadabouts.

The social habits of ants are extremely ancient, having approached perfection at least sixty million years ago. These ways of life seem to change surprisingly little as the centuries go by.

The young of other animals seem far more different from our own, and their parents react to them in unlike social ways.

Furry Creatures

In contrast to the ants is the newborn baby antelope, which is sociable in a family way. It struggles to its feet just forty-five seconds after escaping from its mother's womb. Five minutes after birth, it can run and keep up with her as she tries to avoid a predator. If she must go off to feed herself, her youngster heeds her signal to hug the ground and stay motionless, reducing its chance of being detected.

No mother antelope will allow any calf except her own to nurse, and if it fails to stay close to its sole source of nourishment, it weakens from hunger in a few days. Unintentional separation explains why fewer than half of the antelope calves born in any year survive to their first birthday.

Each pronghorn antelope family works together efficiently, showing a first step toward a monogamous relationship. After the breeding season the male's sexual ardor cools, but he remains with his four or five females (does). Those of his harem take turns watching over the calves while the buck tries to protect the whole group until the calves are weaned and go off on their own. Not until then does the buck concentrate on feeding, building up reserves of energy to use in the winter months and during an ensuing mating season. Surviving calves will have learned to detect and run from danger. The best-nourished female calves may be ready to mate when one year old. A surprising number of them give birth the following summer.

Pronghorns and other mammals that eat plant foods find what they need without having to learn to subdue it as any predator must with active prey. No one should be surprised that young predators take longer to develop than planteaters, time during which they can learn how to survive in their world. The biggest and most ferocious of North American predators, the grizzly bears of Alaska, may still be nursing their cubs at four years of age, while the cubs become adept at securing a meal at the expense of a caribou calf or a wild sheep or even a half-grown moose. Each cub already has the power to overcome its prey but not yet the skills it needs to succeed whenever hungry.

What transformations each individual must undergo from the moment of conception to achievement of maximum competence! First comes the conquest of the egg by the sperm and the fusion of two packets of heredity into a potentially winning combination. Soon, in most mammals, comes the need for the ball-like mass of cells that is the embryo to invade the wall of its mother's womb and supplement the food supply she incorporated in her egg. The embryo generally extends a part of itself with an outlying mesh of its own blood vessels to form a placenta. In this the intact vessels of the embryo come extremely close to the mother's blood, and between the two circulations move water and foodstuffs such as sugars—also hormones and oxygen—in exchange for carbon dioxide and wastes which the mother can discharge. So secure is the fetus inside its mother that if its inheritance destines it to be a female, she will elaborate in her tiny ovaries all the eggs she will ever need for a lifetime of reproduction—and spares as well. Not until a male embryo is born and grows to puberty will he elaborate the sperms that can make a female pregnant. For some still unknown reasons these microscopic swimming cells and the egg must always be fresh.

We like the conclusion that our friend Sally Carrighar reached as she thought about the disparate roles of the sexes in life:

> It is not a male's world that she lives in, nor a female's world. It is just the world, and the male and female are two self-reliant creatures who share it. They may be together permanently, or very infrequently, but in neither case are they competitors or, of course, enemies. There is room for both in their habitat and enough food for both. They will need each other from time to time, and neither will try to prove himself, or herself, by outstripping or by subduing the other.

She tells, too, of her own discoveries with a captive colony of lemmings in northern Alaska, where they had an abundance of water and food, including the arctic vegetation to which they were accustomed. They had moist earth to dig in, driftwood to climb and chew. They thrived in three enclosures of different sizes, frolicking together and sleeping three or four cuddled together in each nest.

But when Sally Carrighar introduced extra lemmings in any enclosure, the newcomers were accepted amicably up to a maximum number, which differed for each cage. Beyond that population came a factor of crowding, which every lemming present recognized. They began pushing one another and box-ing, trying with fangs bared to get at one another's throats, as though striving to reduce the number to a tolerable level. In the open they might have set off on a spectacular emigration in search of adequate space—as lemmings have been known to do for countless years. Removal of surplus individuals lets the irritability subside. Just one lemming, and any one, young or old, made the critical difference the animals recognized.

Parental Care

Without going so far from home, naturalists have colonies of rodents for study at no expense. Each city has its dumps of trash and garbage, where brown rats (*Rattus norvegicus*) exca-vate burrows in which to raise their young secure from hawks, owls, foxes, and other small predators. Each burrow is separate, a small social unit with limited territory to defend, close to nearly endless supplies of food and water. Hidden away, the baby rats are born neither able to see nor hear. The mother licks clean the young she has just produced and learns their scent or taste, which is largely that of the liquid in which they were immersed before birth. With this same liquid in her mouth she licks her own nipples, which gives her young the cue that here they are to attach themselves, hold on, and suck her milk. Her birth fluids contain substances that induce the attachment of her infants, in which the necessary senses of smell and taste are well developed within minutes after they are born.

Probably the members of each group in a burrow know one another as individuals, with no common colony odor that might distinguish an alien from elsewhere. The introduction of a strange rat of the same species is noticed immediately. In some burrow of its choice, it subjects itself abjectly to inspection. The local rats begin aggressive grooming, which may be followed in about five seconds by an outright fight. Rats that have been reared in isolation find the most resistance to being tolerated. The newcomer receives dozens of body wounds and loses weight. Aliens that have been raised in groups get the least aggressive grooming, engage in no fights, and get few body wounds. They lose half as much weight before being accepted. Least resistance is accorded young intruders.

Female brown rats are smaller and less aggressive than males. During food shortages, they obtain adequate nourishment while the males lose weight by fighting among themselves for the right to feed first. Brown rats show an easy reciprocity and interchange of roles that benefit both sexes, quite unlike the one-sided and uneasy truce between the sexes that is characteristic of so many other mammals. The social arrangement among wild primates calls for dominant males to eat first and monopolize any choice or preferred foods. Females in lion prides eat only after the adult males have fed, even when the lioness was responsible for the kill. Their unweaned cubs frequently succumb to starvation when hunting is poor. Rats may be despised, but they are more efficient than lions at protecting and providing for their young.

The most devoted paternal care is shown not by primates but by the African bush dogs. Fathers not only stay close as their pups are born but sometimes pull the young from the birth canal and eat the afterbirth, then lick each pup and learn its scent as a family member to be accorded the utmost of protection.

We think of the male lion, the African "King of Beasts," as roaring and fighting to protect the females and young that constitute his family pride. But when a male outsider from beyond the group manages to defeat the dominant lion and take over his pride, the newcomer generally kills every cub he finds, as though aware that they are not his offspring. Months later cubs he has fathered will be born, and these he will protect with all his power. Cubs with parents hunt all night, sleeping until sunset, when they awake and play.

We are more sympathetic to the way in which parents of the cat family and wild dogs, such as foxes and wolves, lead their young on hunting expeditions as soon as the kittens or pups are old enough to leave the den. The mother may be the principal teacher, or a whole wolf pack may participate. So long as the mother gets enough to eat for her young and herself, she is tolerant of those occasions when the youngsters alarm the potential prey she is stalking and it escapes. If she suffers from poor hunting and hunger herself, she may insist that her young remain in the den while she hunts alone. Later they will be more cautious, and she will demonstrate how to catch the meaty food all of them need.

3

Felines and Their Prey

So many America homes include a pet kitten or, after it grows up, a cat that this pet is more familiar than any other. A kitten weighing only a few ounces seems helpless after its mother licks its fur dry after birth. Its eyes still need another 10 days of development before they open and allow sight. The baby cat has been developing for only 62 days inside its mother, compared to the 250 to 285 days usual for a human baby. Yet the kitten can right itself if turned upside down, can extend its claws, and can cling tightly to a support. It can hear well and respond to its mother's purring sound by relaxing as though it had nothing to fear. It needs to learn her distinctive body odor and to be able to distinguish this scent from that of any other female cat. Unless very hungry it may be reluctant to nurse at the nipples of a substitute mother or even its own, if her underside has been carefully washed and dried.

We may wonder if, when a kitten gets its eyes open, its view differs from that of a few weeks later when the blue film over its eyes disappears, leaving them clear, often golden. Seemingly the change comes so gradually that the kitten's sight adjusts to familiar objects in its world.

From the very beginning, unless it is a member of the Siamese cat breed, a kitten's eyes have a slit pupil which can open wide in dim light and close almost completely if the daylight is bright. In this respect the kitten resembles its presumed ancestors, the Libyan desert cats of North Africa. Thousands of years ago, the Egyptians apparently adopted some kittens of Libyan desert cats as pets with real value: This human society had learned to store grain for seasons when food was hard to find. The stored grain attracted far too many hungry mice from the surrounding country—small animals that a cat could eliminate. A cat, moreover, was a tidy pet, keeping itself clean and allowing children or adults to stroke its soft fur, or disappearing outside the house for days on hunting expeditions if life inside became too stressful. Later the cat would reappear in time to gain shelter from a rainstorm or other adverse weather. The few times the kitten or the cat scratched or bit were excused as permissible self-defense.

A mother cat, after finding her home site unsuited for her kittens, picks them up in her mouth one at a time by the loose skin at the back of their necks and carries them to some substitute location. That the kittens do not make a sound while being transported seems particularly appropriate. This silent behavior of the kitten is an inherited feature, far better for saving life than the wail of a child under conditions of similar stress. Many a human mother, striving to keep her baby safe from warriors invading her community during a military action, has tried in vain to silence her child while sharing its terror of the unfamiliar and unknown.

The Siamese cat, for which no wild Asiatic ancestor is known has eyes with a circular pupil like those of the big cats—the lion, leopards, and tiger. Because these big cats have additional anatomical differences in their throats, they can roar but not purr, whereas the small cats purr and cannot roar. These differences lead scientists to separate the big cats into the genus *Panthera*, distinct from the small cats of genus *Felis*. The house cat is *Felis domestica* wherever it chances to live, the lion *Panthera leo*.

Soon after a kitten has its eyes open, it begins to pursue and play with small objects that move. No parent or person needs to teach the kitten this behavior, for it is inborn. A tuft of cotton tied to the end of a string becomes a target to be pounced on and held still. A ball less than two inches in diameter is something to swat and follow, to stop and divert, with muscular movements similar to those the cat will use to catch a lively mouse. Play becomes a learning experience we can recognize as practice toward the serious task of getting enough prey to eat. Two kittens play together even more roughly, sharpening their reflexes toward the time when each kitten will be on its own. Coordination between eyes/ears and feet/claws is so important that the kitten/cat may seem reluctant to kill and eat what is has caught. Instead, it chooses to extend its practice. It prolongs the chase by pretending to release the victim so long as it is able to move even a little on its own, only to strike it down again and again. A well-fed kitten may disdain a small corpse, maintaining its predatory role without becoming a scavenger.

All of these behaviors, so familiar in the kitten of a domesticated cat, appear with equal importance in the wild long-tailed cat known variously as cougar, mountain lion, painter, panther, and puma. Until recently this was the world's most widespread member of the cat family—at home from Alaska to Patagonia, from Atlantic to Pacific coast. Primarily a forest animal, it prefers to hide its kittens in rocky caves. Like the parents, the young have long thick tails, that of the adult accounting for three of the body's overall nine-foot length. Born with conspicuous black spots, unlike the parent's uniform yellowish-brown short fur, the one to five kittens in a litter have sealed eyes for their first eight or nine days. Their teeth appear at eighteen days, but they do not begin crawling around in the den before age seven weeks. Two weeks later, their attentive parents bring them fresh meat on which to suck, but they are not given meat on which they wean themselves until they are three or four months old. They have a lot to learn to become proficient hunters and accompany their mother into their second year of life. By then she will be attracting a mate and starting a new family, in need of bolstering her own nutrition toward her coming months of gestation and nursing of her next kittens.

Sleep Cycles

When nothing is happening in the vicinity of a kitten or a cat of any kind, the animal relaxes and takes a catnap. Its ears retain their sensitivity, flicking if barely brushed against by a down-arching head of grass moved by a slight breeze. Alertness to any sound continues, although the animal may ignore, as it will not when wide awake, a tickling sensation from the pads of its feet. If a hand strokes its fur, it may open its eyes slightly to identify the person and purr a few times as though appreciating attention. For a stranger it opens its eyes wider and keeps them watchful. Learning who to trust is part of survival.

Sleep as the opposite of wakefulness changes as a kitten or a human baby gets older. Left on its own, a young kitten sleeps soundly for only twenty or thirty minutes before it awakens for new activity. Its sleep cycle progressively extends until, in mature cats, it lasts thirty to forty minutes. A human infant

usually stays in sound sleep for fifty to sixty minutes, gradually extending this time to eight or ninety minutes. Each day the
newborn may get fourteen to fifteen hours of sleep, reducing
this to thirteen to fourteen hours by age six months. The parents may feel that their child is always sleepy, its schedule
hard to synchronize with their own sleeping schedule of seven
to nine hours asleep in each twenty-four.

At first the infant sleeps whenever no distractions prevent
it. A baby that has had its full forty weeks of development in
the womb needs only a few weeks more to consolidate several
short naps into one long night's sleep. After a few days a child
adjusts to sleeping more at night than in the daytime.
Supplementary naps by day may be down to two at age six
months and to one by the end of the first year. Children, like
young animals, need much uninterrupted rest asleep after a
long active day. Those hours allow redistribution of energy
from food into storage sites where it can be called upon quickly as needed the following day.

Nor is the depth of sleep regular, as though some switch
were turned off and on allowing consciousness. Sleep goes
through at least four different stages, each corresponding to
distinctive patterns in brain waves—electrical variations that
can be picked up on the head surface and amplified for
recording on the moving paper tape of an electroencephalo-
graph. The dozing First Stage differs from wakefulness in
showing voltage fluctuations higher than while awake. They
come in bursts of nine to thirteen per second. A sudden twitch
by the muscles of an arm or leg may signal the transition from
semiconsciousness to Second Stage sleep. At this point the
brain waves increase in amplitude of voltage variations and
decrease in frequency. Within about twenty minutes, Second
Stage gives way to Third, with large, slow waves, about one
per second, and a voltage five times that of the initial condition in First Stage. Just a few minutes later, the sleeper enters

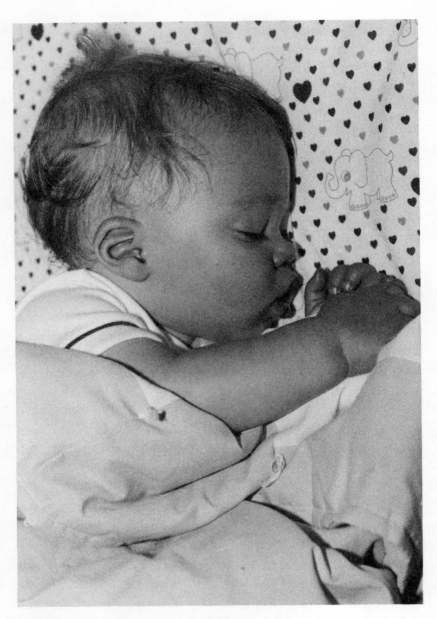

The human baby, like the animal baby, sleeps at first when no distractions prevent it. A baby that has had its full forty weeks of development within the womb needs only a few weeks more to consolidate several short naps into one long night's sleep. (Courtesy of Anne McShane, Barrington, New Hampshire)

Fourth Stage, from which awakening is most resisted. Children reach Fourth Stage faster than adults and spend more minutes there before retracing the changes back through Third, Second, and First, perhaps to wake up. During Fourth Stage sleep, a kitten or a child can be lifted and carried to bed without awakening or remembering the event. During Fourth Stage sleep, the pituitary gland beneath the brain pours into the bloodstream the important growth hormone that stimulates development throughout the body and also adjustments we recognize as early aging. In the human adult, Fourth Stage sleep is briefer, and the return to First Stage usually seems complete in sixty to ninety minutes. Dreams and rapid movements of the eyes beneath their closed lids continue, giving this stage its special name of REM (Rapid Eye Movement) sleep. At the corresponding stage a cat may extend and withdraw its claws, a dog act as though suppressing a chase after some elusive target. It is easy to assume that these pets dream too, but we have no way to find out, even though their brain waves suggest that this may well be true.

Sleep is so puzzling that we should not be surprised to find that conditions suitable for this routine time-out phase of life differ so greatly among members of the animal kingdom. A jumpy rabbit or hare naps briefly in whatever cover it can find, always ready to dash off if signs of danger reach it. A prairie dog, as a burrowing ground squirrel, carries grass into its underground chambers as bedding on which to lie all night. By day, a well-fed prairie dog may take a nap in the sun close to its home doorway, depending on alert members of its community to give a warning bark if a predator is seen.

Big Cats

Lion cubs are more on their own, because the lion and lionesses in the pride offer help only while they are well fed. Cubs must trail after their mothers and others as best they can, alert to any sign that a kill is imminent. The pride does most of its hunting at night, when the keen hearing and soft-footed approach of the big cats compensate for their difficulty in seeing potential prey. Scent is rarely important to these hunters, which may explain why they make so little attempt to remain downwind from their quarry. Often the zebras, wildebeests, or other antelopes they are stalking recognize a lion odor on the breeze and run off to some safer location. An electrical storm during the night, with plenty of lightning and thunder, helps the lioness with light to see by and distracts her targets until it is too late for an escape.

When a kill is made, the mature animals compete for their shares as vigorously as their separate strengths allow. Cubs may stay aside until the victim has been torn apart and the older lions have carried off individual pieces to devour in solitude. Cubs then can have what is left, if not driven away by hyenas at night or by vultures in daylight. Cubs must persist if they are to get enough to eat. Only by being well nourished and strong can they compete toward a future. For their first three months after birth they depend on their mother's milk. But barely half of the cubs born reach maturity.

Sometimes the correct approach toward subduing a potential meal requires the cubs to learn from their mother or an older member of the pride. The prey may be an African porcupine emerging from its burrow after dark. Because it presents thousands of barbed quills, it must be examined with restraint until it can be flipped on its back, exposing its unprotected belly. A cub will doubtlessly get a faceful of quills before discovering on its own how to manage a porcupine.

Any cub that gets injured has extra difficulties because stronger members of the pride will bully it, slowing it as it struggles to keep up with the adults as they hunt. Fortunately,

A male lion, the King of Beasts, shows family pride and will protect his young with all his power. (Courtesy of Satour, South Africa Tourist Corporation)

lion wounds heal rapidly, and a cub that recovers regains its place in the hierarchy. It still heeds loud roars from lions as they seek to join the lionesses in the pride, for lions commonly kill whatever cubs are present and confiscate any foods the lionesses have gathered. When lions arrive, the cubs must hide promptly. Usually they lie down inconspicuously as though resting, which is normal enough for lions of any age. Or they stay close to the lionesses, who tend to avoid the arrival of lions. This may mean traveling together through the dark in the hours before dawn for five to ten miles to find a place in which to relax.

Ordinarily, lions are on their feet and active less than four hours out of each twenty-four, which gives them plenty of time for sleep. The hardest part of a lion's life is surviving the first five years to reach adulthood. Luck, too, is needed for an unprotected kitten to become a cat.

On all sides of the Northern Hemisphere, night-active cats with short, black-tipped tails and a tuft of black bristles on each ear are known as lynxes. So alert and sharp-sighted are they that Europeans in 1609 named their first scientific society the Academy of the Lynx. Each of these cats matures at a body length of three feet and a weight of forty pounds. In America, its success depends almost entirely on the abundance or scarcity of snowshoe hares, whose numbers vary from one hundred to the acre down to virtually none. Ernest Thompson Seton used his connections in the Hudson's Bay Company to learn from their records how many hare pelts and how many lynx skins their traders had purchased from 1821 through 1908. Disease almost wipes out the hare population every nine to ten years, and lynxes starve. While the few surviving hares benefit from untouched food and multiply prodigiously, lynx numbers rise again, although more slowly. In Canada, according to Seton, the lynx "follows the Hares, thinks Hares, tastes like Hares, increases with them, and on their failure dies of starvation in the unrabbited woods."

In good years, a mother lynx may produce four tiny kittens in a den under a hollow log. She weans them two months later and has her mate's help in supplying them with solid food for the dozen months while they live with her. Undisturbed and adequately nourished, a lynx can survive for a dozen years, exploiting a territory fifty miles across. Over much of this area the mother nurtures her bouncy kittens' inborn instinct to pounce on anything that moves. She takes them with her on hunting trips and waits when one wails because it has lagged behind. The lynx's undoing is its need for unpeopled wilderness, and it has disappeared everywhere that the world is no longer wild.

One size smaller than the lynx and far more tolerant of land where people live is the American wildcat. Maturing at close to forty pounds, and forty inches from nose tip to the end of the six-inch, white-tipped tail, the male strides along while yowling the most spine-tingling calls of the year. Sometimes a second male responds, and the two provide a duet followed by sounds of battle so loud and ferocious as to make a fight between tomcats seem a sham.

The male wildcat leaves his pregnant mate of the moment, with no concern for the one to four kittens born about sixty-three days later. Unless her den is discovered, she will return to it and feed her nurslings until they are about two months old. She weans them while teaching them to hunt. Until autumn, when the kittens weigh about twelve pounds each and become independent, she will defend her family against a dog or coyote. Thereafter they must find their own cottontails, jackrabbits, unwary rodents (including squirrels), and birds. Plant foods account for about 16 percent of the wildcat's diet. More than two-thirds of the remainder is meat of mammals that are harmful to human interests.

In most of Africa and southern Europe, people show little concern for the welfare of wild animals that might be helpful. They seem too preoccupied with human affairs to notice that the fastest mammal on earth is facing hard times. The cheetah or "hunting leopard" must be able to watch from short grassy areas until a herd of small antelopes, zebra with some young foals, or other potential prey comes close. From a distance of about two hundred yards, the cheetah is unsurpassed in dashing after its chosen victim, striking with a forepaw the hind legs of the target and pouncing on its neck before the fallen creature can get up again. If she has hidden her cubs close by, a mother cheetah may drag a small catch back to them or call her young to come and feast before some other predator takes away the prize.

For no known reason, adult cheetahs are easier to tame than their cubs, which are born blind in tall grass and open their eyes in four to eleven days. Weighing less than half a pound at birth, they grow at modest speed and are walking about erratically after a week. At three weeks their first teeth appear, and they are eager to follow their mother or run ahead of her. She makes a little purring sound, to which they respond *peep-peep* and hurry back. She weans them at five months, but their adult teeth do not develop until they are eight months old. As they mature, the three to six cubs in a litter play even more vigorously but fail to entice their sedate parent from her vigil in watching for suitable prey. For her, being fast is not enough. Spectacular bursts of speed tire her quickly, and she often fails to catch a meal. Even when she succeeds, a leopard, a lion, a hyena, or a group of vultures may chase her away before she can share the meat with her cubs.

Cheetahs, especially the females, are completely asocial, excluding the cubs that live with them. They make a living in a very large home range, on the order of 800 square kilometers in the Serengeti, because they follow the migratory habits of their favorite prey, Thomson's gazelle. They are not territorial and are unable to cover so large a range, so they share sections of their hunting area with several other females at any one time. This relative concentration of females is enough to make it worthwhile for several males to join forces to defend these loose aggregations against other males so as to monopolize mating opportunities. The males live in small coalitions and the females do not, so there is no equivalent to a pride of lions.

But the asocial female cheetahs do not live alone, according to Tom Caro of the University of Michigan. He has shown that for more than three-quarters of their lives, female cheetahs live in the company of their cubs, which usually number three in the Serengeti population. And for at least half of this time the cubs are big enough and have sufficiently large appetites that the food demands of her litter far exceed her own. Although

Cheetah females are considered asocial, yet for more than three quarters of their lives, they live in the company of their cubs, which usually number three in the Serengeti population. (Courtesy of Satour, South Africa Tourist Corporation)

the cubs learn to hunt with their mother, for the most part they contribute very little to their upkeep: "Cubs appear to be essentially parasitic on adult females for food."

By living in larger groups in company with other mothers, female cheetahs would have to increase the volume of food production. They would have more failed chases than successful ones. They would have to do more hunting. Given the other caretaking activities the mothers must perform, this would leave about seven-and-a-half minutes of "free time" in each hour.

Because of the constraints under which female cheetahs currently hunt, they need to be able to exploit larger prey that are easy to catch. Such prey either do not exist or are very scarce. Nor is this option available to most felids. Lions can hunt large prey and therefore can be social. But for the rest of the cats, the costs of hunting keeps them asocial.

Belgian-born Armand Davis tells of "four precious cheetah kittens" offered to him on a farm in Kenya, where he regards them as "the most beautiful of all young cats." Covered at first with long, rather soft, blue-gray hair on the back, with the rest of the body tawny brown with solid dark spots, they make many sounds: growling, snarling, spitting, mewing, and purring almost like a house cat. Adults produce little birdlike chirps and, when pursued, give up running and are easily captured. Tamed cheetahs show interest in affection. Generally they are believed to be free of unreliable behavior such as is expected of other big cats when domesticated.

When we asked Mr. C. A. van Ee, director of the Bloemfontein Zoo in South Africa, whether a cheetah's fur is as stiff as it appears, he insisted we follow him into the cage where several alert adult animals were housed. He alarmed us by seizing one 130-pound animal by its 2 1/2 foot tail, curling this around a metal stanchion supporting the mesh of the cage roof, and inviting us to finger the back fur of the four-foot animal he held so unceremoniously. It offered no real resistance, and its fur *was* bristly stiff, less than half an inch thick, and somewhat longer along the back of its neck. The cheetah made no audible sound and, when released, simply joined others in the cage along the farther side, away from the door through which we could emerge.

Now we can understand why Mesopotamians, Egyptians, Minoans, and nobles in southern Europe and most recently in India chose to train adult cheetahs as hunting companions. The long-legged slender cat would ride in a cart or behind a horseman like the passenger on a motorcycle, often perched on a pillow, perhaps blindfolded until needed to run down some hare, bighorned ewe, or other member of the deer family.

Cats' Prey

On a mountainside, bighorn rams snooze on craggy slopes but waken intermittently to test the air and quickly look around for hazards they could avoid. The bighorn ewe seeks solitude when her lambs or twins are due to be born. In some secluded spot under a jutting ledge or atop a talus slope at the foot of a cliff, she watches for danger. An hour later she is on her feet, standing guard while her young totter on shaky legs to reach the nipples below her udder. Even to drink or find some food she goes no more than a few steps from the nursery area. She must be ready to bound back and stand above her offspring lest a golden eagle swoop down to snatch a meal. For a week or so the ewe keeps her new family to herself. Then she trusts the lambs to follow her as she rejoins the herd, where the food supply is more adequate.

By age one month, a lamb has grown so much it must kneel to nurse. Its horns appear at two months. Female lambs grow much more slowly than males, although the ewe suckles both equally until they are about six months old and can be weaned. The female lamb at one year is considerably smaller than a male of equal age. He continues to develop physically and change toward adult behavior until he is seven to nine years old. By then, on a good diet, he may weigh five hundred pounds and stand forty-two inches tall at the shoulder. His massive horns will be curling toward a complete circle, whereas those on ewes of the same age will be gently curving spikes. She will have retained her gregarious nature, while his will have largely disappeared.

Among each hundred mature ewes on the mountain there may be seventy lambs a month after they were born. Half of them may be lost before they are weaned. By one year of age, the number of young has typically fallen to around fifteen. In many areas, the mortality rate is higher because the sheep descend for the winter into mountain valleys and onto adjacent plains where domestic sheep have devoured the vegetation and been hauled away. Malnutrition and diseases now limit bighorn populations where, in the past, they faced predators more often. Lambs that played too much tag and could not keep up with the adults in mountain country lagged behind and fell easy prey to wolves. So did old sheep, weakened after their teeth broke or wore loose, which prevented the animals from cutting and grinding their food effectively.

Mountain goats graze and doze on many of the same high mountain slopes. At all seasons they prefer alpine grasses and sedges as food. To reach these plants the goats step carefully, yet rarely do they fall or slip, even when buffeted by winds or pelted by hail and snow. If a narrow ledge ends, the goat rises on its hind legs with its belly toward the mountain and twists around to walk back the way it came. Even the he-goats, which roam from one family group of nannies and kids to another, battle with other males, mostly by show rather than with sharp-tipped horns. Where a misstep can carry an oppo-

Bighorn lambs have horns that appear at two months. Female lambs grow much more slowly than males although the ewe suckles both equally until they are about six months old and can be weaned. (Courtesy of Charles G. Hansen, Bureau of Sports Fisheries and Wildlife)

nent downslope to death, actual fighting is too hazardous. He is circumspect, too, in his approach to a nanny goat until she becomes truly receptive. She will bear her kid the following spring while on her way upslope to summer range. By then her mate will be on ahead in a bachelor group of three or four, aiming for still higher ground.

The nanny goat stops momentarily by herself in a minimal shelter to drop her kid, which will be on its feet and nursing in minutes. After it has its first meal, she forces it to lie down while she gets herself something to eat. It leaps up when she returns and may try jumping about in a stiff-legged way within thirty minutes of being born. The nanny does her best to stand over her offspring or to bleat softly, summoning it back to her if it strays. Not for several days will she rejoin the little herd she left to give birth and introduce her kid to the other nannies and their playful families. Some family groups include yearlings that are still following their mothers.

A mother hare barely stops traveling to give birth. When the moment comes, she raises herself by extending her hind legs almost vertically, and the baby slides out in its protective sac. She turns slightly and cuts the sac open with her teeth. The youngster crawls out, with both eyes open. The mother eats the sac and licks her baby until it is clean and dry. Then she hops ahead, and the newborn hare runs after her. She stops to let it nurse a while. Within minutes, a second baby is ready to be born, and she repeats her procedure. The hare's entire litter, which may number from three to eight, makes its appearance within half an hour, and the mother will have moved twenty to thirty yards farther along her path from the place where her first baby was born. Every youngster follows close behind her, waiting for another chance to get some milk.

Unlike common rabbits, hares make no burrows, no nests, of any kind. By the time a young hare is a week old, it can raise its ears and hop. Before the end of the next week, it is sampling some of the same plants its mother eats. By contrast, a young rabbit of equal age will still be in a fur-lined nest, not yet ready to open its eyes for the first time. Even when fully grown, a rabbit's legs are never as long as those that carry a hare forward at such great speeds. And only the hare grows a breadth of bristly hairs upon its large hind feet, which leave a mark in the snow suggesting the imprint of snowshoes. That is why the hare so often is called the "snowshoe hare" or the "snowshoe rabbit" by people who are unaware of the difference.

A mother hare takes few chances with her babies until they are old enough to be independent. She leaves them individually in locations she regards as safe while she hops off to browse or rushes at top speed to elude some pursuer. When her stomach is full and the way seems clear, she returns to each youngster and lets it nurse in its hideaway. A baby hare weighs about a quarter of a pound at birth and gains about half an ounce every day. Within a month it will wander off, completely on its own. It will show no sign of recognizing its own mother if it meets her elsewhere on her territory. After all, she is not the only hare in the ten-acre area. Other adult hares visit because their homelands overlap, and their youngsters, too, will be exploring, to get used to the location of obstacles and food. Snowshoe hares find what they need in many places between the Pacific and Atlantic oceans and as far north as there are trees. A northern tract of spruce and fir with boggy areas suits them just as well as a thicket of swampy land somewhat farther south.

Male hares cover more ground than females and try to find a female as soon as she gives birth. The female is willing to mate again once she has cleaned and fed the last of her litter. This explains why she can produce three litters of young each summer at less than six-week intervals. Only the first courtship of the year seems more of a game, with the female leading the male on a merry chase through the forest, dodging him and spurning his advances. From March into April, she refuses to let him catch her, or she kicks and bites at him if he comes too close. Suddenly, she is ready and accepts any male approaching her until her mood changes.

In autumn the hares seem more subdued. They are too busy eating, adding to their reserves of fat, to show much interest in other activities. Winter is coming. A fat hare has nourishment to live on while storms rage. Snow offers no real hazard. The snowshoe hare can walk on top of all but the most powdery snow. The white covering over the earth serves, in fact, as an elevator. It raises the hare to levels of branches and bark that it could not reach while standing, even tiptoe, on the ground.

A young hare needs months of experience to learn whether it must run for its life or can remain safe merely by staying completely still. It takes months to train itself to leap ahead of a pursuer without crashing into some obstacle. During these months, many a young hare becomes a meal for a bobcat, lynx, fox, coyote, or, in some places, a wolf. At night, the hare may be pounced on silently by a great horned owl or a great gray owl. Consequently, only about thirty out of every one hundred young hares survive to their first birthday. The thirty survivors mature but still face many dangers. Fifteen of them disappear before they are two years old, and eight will be lucky to reach age three. Rarely do more than four live to their fourth birthday. Two may be left at five years after birth.

Hares have no way to protect their young and themselves from diseases or to find real safety from birds and beasts of prey. They gain what security is possible by staying close to home, in familiar territory. They never get lost. Rarely does one die from starvation, for there is food all around it; yet each move to get something to eat exposes the hare to danger. Escaping is its way of life.

4

Leaving the Nest

Seldom is it wise to come between a mother bear and her young cub. She will attack if she sees no way to get her youngster to safety. And to a mother bear, safe means up a sturdy tree. One warning cough is all she has to make if the tree is near. Her cub scrambles immediately, even though this puts it into clear view from all around.

Once her cub is old enough to be allowed outside the den where it was born, she need not teach it to climb. Its climbing muscles develop so quickly that, in an emergency recognized by its mother, a cub will climb quite readily. Hours or minutes later, the cub must back down without falling, while no longer able to see where its feet are going. It has no rear-view mirrors and may easily find itself astraddle a sturdy side branch that was bypassed without problems on the upward trip. Nor can its mother tell it what to do. If the cub waits too long to reach the ground, she may even wander off to search for food, as though unconcerned that her cub may never find her for another meal of milk. Whining sounds from the hungry youngster do not carry far in woodland, and the energy in her gruff voice is absorbed quickly by tree bark even if she tries to give direction.

All of this behavior is programmed in the bear's inheritance. The cubs, as many as four, undergo their birth while their mother is still groggy toward the end of her annual hibernation. Her young weigh only a half pound each—the size of a guinea pig—and must find their way to her milk, never to leave her until she leads them from her den. With luck they will learn from her all summer—how to get edible ants and beetles, what berries to eat—and be weaned in autumn when it is time for them to find or dig their own den sites. Each cub acts as though it would rather play than heed its mother's teaching.

Occasionally a baby has to decide which is greater, pleasure or pain. Young black bears reach this point in life when they stand near a tree being torn apart by the mother bear to get at honey made by a wild colony of honeybees. The baby and mother both get stung and feel the pain. With luck the baby shares a generous portion of sweet honeycomb, perhaps after the bees cease to defend it as darkness spreads following sundown and the end of twilight. Since each worker bee dies from inflicting its stinger and poison gland on an invader, we can appreciate why this weapon is rarely used in the dark when a hive robber is as invisibly black to them as the forest shade.

The number of honeybees defending their honey during daylight hours is rarely as large as those that gather when other animals are to be discouraged. The odor of a sweaty bear with young clinging to the fur of the big animal conceals the scent of bees sacrificing themselves to the sting of an intruder. This communication among adult honeybees concentrates their mass attack. Only at dusk do some show inde-

With bears, once a cub is old enough to be allowed outside the den, the climbing muscles develop quickly, and no practice is needed to scamper up a tree. (Courtesy of Montana Fish and Game)

pendence, then chiefly by using their tiny jaws to bite down on twigs of shrubs where they will sleep all night, until day once more lets them find their way home. A safer hideaway appeals at dusk to bumblebees, which seek out a cup-shaped flower in which to hide and sleep.

A mother raccoon is also very resourceful, hiding her young in tree cavities to which she has found an access hole. No forest that is well managed has many old dead trees, for the forestry people want all the space in their forest occupied by live plants that are still producing wood. What taxes does the raccoon pay? When the old hickory tree dies after being struck by lightning, no one is likely to give a moment's praise for the raccoon that years ago planted a hickory nut where the agents of decay in soil would rot off the husk and soften the shell, letting the seed inside germinate and produce a tree.

A baby porcupine stays so briefly with its mother that it has little chance to learn much from her. Like a runaway from home, it wanders off just a few days after it is born. At birth its quills are soft, but they harden as soon as they are dry. By then the baby porcupine has its eyes open and reacts to any disturbance by raising its loose quills in self-defense. Already the baby is eleven inches long and has good teeth, including two big orange front teeth in its upper and lower jaws. On its second day it climbs trees to follow its mother. Within a week it goes off on its own, to live the rest of its life on plant foods, such as evergreen needles, the inner bark of trees, water plants, and fleshy fruits. The mother porcupine shows no concern over the future of her single youngster. She has nourished her baby inside her body for sixteen weeks and about a week more on milk. After that she treats it as a stranger if they meet. When the hollow quills have dried and hardened into barb-surfaced spears, the little "porcupet" is thoroughly ready to swat those quills on its tail into the nose of any predator so foolish as to approach from behind.

Under its coat of fur and quills, the body of the porcupine is almost invisible. Except for size, it is hard to tell a young individual from an old one although the shape of the head and the proportions of the toes and of the tail do change as an animal grows. In weight the young porcupine increases from about twenty ounces at birth to around three and a half pounds by the end of its first summer and to eight pounds a year later. When the porcupine matures at the end of its third summer, it usually weighs about twelve pounds and measures twenty-five inches from its nose to the base of its tail; the quill-studded tail adds another five inches. Sometimes a particularly large, old porcupine weighs forty pounds and is thirty-six inches in length. Usually it is a male.

Any porcupine will climb a tree if one is near. A very few old porcupines find a hollow open to the outside, tapering upward to total closure. The animal can wedge its body in such a place and protect both its head and its belly. These are favorite targets of the big tree-climbing member of the weasel family—the fisher—which can flip most porcupines onto their backs and kill them with a few bites into unprotected undersurfaces. Only a porcupine's mate can approach her from behind without harm and then very, very carefully, following her invitation.

In the rain forests of the American tropics live slow-moving sloths of several kinds. They hang much of each day and night beneath horizontal branches by hooking their claws over the branches and seldom moving. The shaggy hair of the sloth blends inconspicuously among the foliage, keeping the animal almost invisible. On the ground it is like a fish out of water, obviously out of place and most vulnerable to predators. Baby sloths are brown, born singly at the beginning of the dry season. Each baby clambers onto its mother's underside, which faces the branch from which she suspends herself. There the youngster has a choice between two nipples and feeds when-

The sloth baby is brown and born singly at the start of the dry season. It clambers onto its mother's underside and hangs upside down until it is weaned and can manage on its own. (Courtesy of Lorus J. Milne and Margery Milne, Durham, New Hampshire)

ever hungry while its mother is asleep or, at night, is reaching for green foliage to eat. During a rain she can relieve herself of wastes without attracting attention. Otherwise, once a week she must climb down to the ground, dig a small hole with her short tail, and discharge her pellets. Her legs are too weak to let her stand upright. She pulls herself along the ground and climbs back up to the forest canopy to continue her slow existence. Her baby just rides along until it is weaned and can manage on its own. By then it has learned to stay still and, without being noticed, hang upside down and let the world go by.

In far-off Australia a koala baby goes up a tree with its

mother, clinging tightly to her shoulders. She provides direction and transport, too. By preference, most of her life is spent high above the ground in eucalyptus trees, where she clings with her hind feet while reaching out for the leaves that comprise her favorite food. In keeping with this head-down posture, the pouch in which the baby koala finds its original refuge opens to the rear, not the front as in a kangaroo and most other marsupial mammals. In fact, a baby koala is believed to gain its acquaintance with eucalyptus leaves from the undigested residues the mother extrudes as waste. Later, when the baby emerges from the pouch and rides on its mother's back, it has opportunity to meet fresh eucalyptus leaves and learn which few among the six hundred species are digestible and which should be left uneaten.

Far more customary among mammals is for the baby at weaning age to reach for food being eaten by the mother and sample items she relies upon. A baby rat learns in this way just a few days after being born. It also shuns in later life any food it has witnessed the mother rejecting. Few lessons seem more important in survival, and usually the baby learns from a single experience.

Sometimes at night, with a flashlight, you can see a mother opossum on a low branch of a tree. She may have ten or more babies riding on her back. Generally she holds her long tapering tail turned up and forward, almost to her head. The babies cling to her fur and also wrap their tails around their mother's tail, which keeps them from falling off. Sometimes they must be hidden while she goes forth alone, much later to return to nurse them. By two months of age, those babies will all be weaned and off on their own. The males will never grow to be as big as their sisters or their mothers. A big female opossum is thirty-six inches long in the body, with an eighteen-inch tail, and weighs about five pounds. If food is plentiful, she may have three litters of young in a year, the first litter in April and the last one in September. The success of opossums in the Temperate Zone is due in large measure to the short time it takes the young to mature, for these animals originated in tropical America and have spread north out of Mexico only during the last thousand years.

5

Canines—Domestic and Wild

Ten thousand years ago someone in central Europe found a litter of wolf cubs and carried them home as playful companions for his child. On a rough diet of foods prepared for people, the cubs grew up, romping and playing as though human children were other canines. This bit of unrecorded history has been repeated many times, such as when naturalist Lois Crisler raised two wolves acquired from Eskimos and found them delightful companions. When five orphaned wolf cubs were introduced into the lives of the maturing wolves, they fed and protected them as though they were their own. Not satisfied to regard the pets as wolves, humankind changed the name of their young to puppy dogs. They grew up to be domesticated animals—the first kind of wild mammal taken into human households.

Selective control over dog breeding separated more than half a dozen unlike kinds in just a few hundred years. Clear drawings of them on cave walls and even some embalmed individuals reveal how descendants of the then-widespread gray wolf, *Canis lupus*, became different under domestication, to become the common dog, *Canis familiaris*.

About fourteen days after the birth of a dog the pup's eyes open and it learns quickly. From its parents it inherits a reluctance to foul its sleeping space. This reluctance can be encouraged to apply to the whole house if each "mistake" is followed right there with a mild rebuke or a gentle swat with a cloth or a newspaper. Once housebroken, the pet keeps itself from making mistakes, perhaps whining to be let outdoors before it is too late, then crying to be allowed back in.

About six weeks after a wolf pup is born, its mother strives to wean it to foods more solid than milk. Her natural procedure calls upon her to regurgitate small amounts of her own food after she has begun to digest it. If the pup does not swallow every bit, she is likely to eat it again herself. This keeps the home box clean and tidy. In the wild she would normally gorge herself on suitable food and regurgitate much of it into a hole dug in the ground near the den, then return to the food supply for another meal. Later, her sensitivity to odors would help her return to her buried store and take from it what she wanted for herself or her young. For an adult wolf a normal meal is about 5.5 pounds daily, which requires the pack to kill annually about fifteen adult white-tailed deer per wolf. On such diets, wolves and their smaller kin, the coyotes and jackals, have been succeeding for thousands of years. Unless actively discouraged by fastidious people, they continue their old habits of overeating and regurgitating when they have young to rear.

A coyote mother insists on being alone while giving birth and suckling her pups in the den. Her mate must find shelter elsewhere for about two months. Then he is welcomed back and given a chance to meet his offspring.

Coyote pups five to six weeks of age are allowed to play at the entrance to the den and to sun themselves there. Their ears are bigger and their eyes smaller than those of dogs of a comparable age. Not until they have two adults looking out for them are they led away on hunting trips and shown how to catch mice or rabbits. At first, the youngsters are awkward, excited, noisy, and completely unable to surprise prey or kill it efficiently. By the time they are experts, autumn has arrived and their parents are rejecting them. No longer can they stay within their parents' territory. At the risk of their lives, they disperse to seek a place of their own. Some find a home more than a hundred miles from where they started out. By the first of the next year, the survivors are mature.

Although a coyote leaves tracks much like those of a dog, the animal itself is seen as a gray shape running across a field or a road. It holds its ears up and forward, its tail low and drooping—not high, as does the much larger wolf. By learning quickly and showing extraordinary skill in adapting to new situations, the coyotes have increased their range and their numbers despite efforts to get rid of them. In some states they have made friends with local dogs, giving rise to "coy-dogs," in which are combined some of the cunning and most of the scavenging habits of the coyote ancestor.

It can be no accident that meat-eaters of the dog family come in several different sets, each with its characteristic body and habits in hunting. Size of predator and of prey go hand in hand. The wolf, weighing up to 80 pounds if female and 150 pounds if male, chooses for itself and its young larger prey than the coyote, weighing no more than 50 pounds. Quite a different diet serves the red foxes and gray foxes, which weigh 12 or 14 pounds. Although the Arctic fox gains weight by preying efficiently on two-ounce lemmings, it frequently loses by being the prey of a neighboring wolf, which might ignore a lemming in the snow.

Arctic foxes go hungry when lemmings become scarce, as they do almost every fourth year in the far north. Unlike the snowy owls, which are their chief competitors for lemmings, the foxes cannot fly south to hunt for other prey. But in bad years, every male that has failed to find a mate may set off southward on foot. Some venture as far as the northern coniferous forests (taiga) across Eurasia and in North America to the nearest fringe of the Canadian prairie provinces and areas of Labrador, which are south of their normal range. Their departure relieves somewhat the danger that pregnant females and attendant males on the home territory will starve before spring. Whether the emigrants ever find their way north again is still unknown. The lucky ones see a polar bear and follow it along a coast—even out onto an ice floe twenty miles from shore. Since the big bear eats only about half of each seal it catches, the fox can feast on remainders.

Less than two months after her February mating, a female Arctic fox gives birth to from six to a dozen young. A few days before they are due, she and her mate find a branching den to "renovate." Digging one in frozen ground is almost impossible. A few pairs are less resourceful. Then the mother is seen rushing about amid the snowdrifts of May, carrying in her mouth a shivering newborn pup or two as she searches for suitable shelter. Without it, the pups—clad only in thin coats of brown fuzzy fur—will never survive the polar winds. Not until autumn do they possess the dense woolly coat that is characteristic of Arctic foxes and the pad of long hairs that keeps their feet insulated from the snow.

A good den is no guarantee for a young fox. Each one will have to fight for a place to nurse if the number of pups is greater than the number of nipples. Weaklings are shoved aside and soon starve to death. Fighting continues when the parents begin the weaning process, bringing home carrion for their youngsters. No more than half of a litter may survive until the milk supply tapers off. Half of the remainder usually perish within a year after birth. The number of two-year-olds is rarely 10 percent of the total that the mothers contributed to that particular year's newborns.

Unlike members of the cat family, dogs show indications of pleasure when they have hard bones to chew. The cat's stomach retains bones and fur or feathers, then wads them into a mass that can be coughed up. The dog's strong jaws expose the central marrow of a bone, where the prey animal used to produce its own red blood cells. Dogs cannot know how nourishing the marrow is, but they obviously want to reach and eat it. Lacking big bones, a pup or growing dog may chew on an odorous old shoe or boot as an acceptable though unrewarding substitute. Most pet stores sell six-inch lengths of rawhide (untanned leather) as lasting, chewable items a young dog will enjoy.

After a dog has followed its human companion on walks around the property where its home is located, the animal learns its boundaries and generally marks them with squirts of urine. These have natural meaning to a strange dog and retain enough odor that the pet marks the same places again and again. Pups that encounter such a warning signal from a large dog may tuck their tails between their legs and run for home as fast as they can. One naturalist who remembered this canine habit put it to good use when he resented the readiness of a wild wolf to invade his campground in the far north. He simply marked his own boundaries in a similar way. Although the task took him all night, he kept on, regretting that he had claimed such a large area; next day he felt rewarded when the wolf respected his signs and stayed beyond them, marking in fifteen minutes every one of his sites with canine urine as the limit of wolf territory, too.

Canine pups are not born with this inner guidance. During the first month, they void their wastes in the nest their mother has prepared for them, and she cleans up every bit, keeping them clean and dry. Thereafter she leads them out, and they learn to rid themselves in some favored spot, returning to it with remarkable regularity. From this age on, they show remarkable interest in wastes, whether their own or those of kin or strangers. Special glands add individual odors to those materials and, using a keen discrimination among these scents, the young canine identifies where it should add markings of its own or run the other way. Scent posts become the canine equivalent of newspapers, telling who came by and left a "calling card."

Trappers are well aware that if they kill a large animal such as a deer or moose, they can protect it from wolves merely by leaving a well-worn jacket spread over the carcass. Smelling the odor of human sweat on the jacket, any wolf that is not actually starving will stay away.

Knowing how tightly organized each wolf pack is on the basis of scent recognition, scientists who attach radio collars to wolves so that they can be followed from a distance have feared that human scent from handling the animal might destroy its acceptability among other members of its pack. But handled wolves return immediately to full acceptance among their kin.

Ordinarily the puppies of a domesticated dog show instant acceptance of people who treat them well. Actually this is a true learning process, for if no person comes near a pup until it is twelve weeks old, it remains shy of people for the rest of its life. Trainability depends on associating with a human caretaker during ages six to eight weeks, learning the scent in context with pleasurable sensations. It reveals how much the animal is striving to understand man, without the counterpart that Albert Schweitzer sought, for "man always to strive to understand the animal." Probably a similar cutoff date applies to children—a time when the child must learn to enjoy some canine association if a warmth is to be shown to dogs in later life. Having a kitten for a pet earlier does not subsequently open an appreciative door for any dog.

Cats and dogs have an inside track toward acceptability as pets, even though they are incapable of responding with words to human speech directed at them. Probably we communicate with dogs by visual cues more than we realize. Slight movements and quick glances may do the trick, in a system the animals use among themselves. Our physician insists that dogs communicate by eye and that a visitor's dog will enter his living room without hesitation only if he blindfolds the springer spaniel at his feet by the fireplace. Does the strange dog receive a warning from the eyes of the physician's dog, or does the springer—unless blindfolded—react to the arrival of the visitor's dog with some slight movement the newcomer detects?

Many modern anthropologists now compare the development of social behavior in a child with that of a newborn wolf pup protected and taught by members of the pack. As in the wolf pack, the young depend on older individuals—often a parent or a relative—to provide the care that is so essential to proper development. Each youngster seems alert to the present and unconcerned about the past or future. It enjoys a kind of security most adults miss.

Among wolves, only one litter of pups is born to the pack each year: the offspring of the dominant ("alpha") male and his mate (the "alpha female"). The rest of the pack are inhibited from breeding, to become equivalent to uncles and aunts, actively involved with nurturing the young of their leaders—helping them to stay healthy, to grow and learn.

As in human families, either parent can take the dominant role, or some other related individual can serve as a replace-

Puppies of a domesticated dog show instant acceptance of people who treat them well. It is a true learning process because if no person comes near it as a pup, it remains shy of people. Trainability depends on associating early with a human caretaker. (Courtesy of Anne McShane, Barrington, New Hampshire, and Lainie Beede-Harvey, Dover, New Hampshire)

ment—a surrogate mother or father. The youngster may experience some difficulty transferring trust to a different caretaker, while the new care-giver gains confidence in being able to provide what the baby needs. The child noticeably gains strength while the other is near and attentive.

Toward members of their own kind, wolves show a whole spectrum of reactions. Individuals that have grown up in the same pack engage in endless games of tag and bouts of wrestling with no attempt to use their powerful jaws in harmful biting. One wolf may seize another by the scruff of the neck or try to get hold of the other's jaw as each lunges at the other with mouth wide open. Some of these sessions of rough play are almost silent. Occasionally, the competitors growl or bark softly in excitement.

A real growl is a final warning to move off. A mother may produce it if playful youngsters come too close to her small pups. A few sharp barks, loud and clear, stop every wolf, no matter what it is doing, and cause it to listen alertly and discover what the danger is. A howl, particularly at night, is generally a sign that all is well but that strangers should stay away—beyond hearing distance. In howling, each wolf adds its own personal harmonics, which other wolves of the pack recognize.

When a strange wolf approaches a pack, it comes slowly and hesitantly. The pack members face the new arrival with steady stares and a distinctive body language that every wolf understands. Suspicion and potential hostility become evident when the hairs on head and back are raised, the tail extends horizontally, and the muscles below the skin of the face contract in special patterns. Responding to this display, the stranger ordinarily lowers its head, droops its tail abjectly, and turns its head away. It avoids looking any pack member in the eye. If the members of the pack approach the newcomer, it lies down, finally rolling over with feet up and belly vulnerable, letting itself be inspected at close range. The more submissive and juvenile the stranger can appear, the more likely the pack is to tolerate it as an addition to the wolf population in their territory. The slightest gesture of self-assertion starts a fight, in which the pack may allow the newcomer no chance to escape alive.

The extreme in submission is that shown by a pup that lies on its back, passively allowing its mother to cleanse it however she chooses. "Active submission" is the behavior of a pup that approaches to beg for milk or food. Each newcomer to a pack must act in these ways even after it has been provisionally accepted. And in any wolf hierarchy, low members are always ready to show submissive posture if they are challenged by any higher member.

The alpha male and his lifelong mate meet every challenge to their status. Particularly in the March breeding season, they become so protective that they effectively limit the courtship activity of all inferior wolves. Only the distraction of abundant prey seems to loosen these limitations and allow all of the mature wolves to reproduce at close to their maximum rate. Then the natural increase in the population may rise to 20 or 30 percent annually. Even this gain may be curtailed if the supply of food decreases after pregnancies begin. Until the embryos become firmly implanted in the walls of the womb, the mother is likely to absorb them as useless tissue if her hunger grows acute. Newborn pups suffer and may die if their mothers must go off to hunt because her usually attentive mate cannot find a surplus to bring back to the den. Others in the pack will also be too hungry to serve as baby-tenders, for they must range widely in search of food. How many of these behaviors arose among members of humankind during the millennia when our ancestors banded together with more characteristics of wolves than of any other mammals?

In *The Wolves of Mount McKinley*, Dr. Adolph Murie tells of two days when grizzly bears came upwind, attracted by the smell of meat and of wolf pups in a den. First a mother bear (sow) with three two-year-old cubs tried vainly to get at the young wolves. Four adult wolves, "at home" ready to defend the young, were equally ferocious in keeping the bears at bay. The next day another monstrous bear came through and had to be kept moving.

The bear did not touch any of the wolves, although once the black-mantled male escaped from the bear's outstretched arms only by strenuous efforts. On this occasion, at least, the wolves surely discouraged the bear with their spirited attack.

One of the protecting wolves may have been the father of the young in the den. But had he any way to know this? More likely, all adult wolves feel responsibility for the immature, which need protection. The mute impulse saves the lives of individuals that carry the seeds of the future. Psychologist and philosopher Ira Progoff claims that the animals' instincts are "not for self-preservation but for life-preservation."

6

Bat Habits

A surprising array of parents safeguard their young by carrying them about. As the babies grow, they become unwelcome burdens, which must be left to wait until their parents return with food. This places special demands on both young and old.

Little bats, for example, are born with wings but not with the strength and ability to fly. At first a mother bat may carry her baby with her while she flits through the night in search of insects to eat. Then the weight and bulk of her baby gets too great, and she leaves it at home in her roosting area. Before dawn, she returns many times to nurse her infant, for, like a human newborn, it needs milk every few hours. Each time she returns, the sound of her voice triggers an outburst of calls from her youngster, and she hones in on it to give it its meal. Seldom will a mother bat nurse any youngster except her own, which makes it essential that baby and mother bat get together with a minimum of lost time. Babies other than her own will try to take advantage of a chance to nurse.

When you think of the thousands or millions of baby bats clinging to the wall of a cave or to the inside of a hollow tree or some space in a building, you understand how impatient each baby gets as it waits for its mother to return. Automatically she comes first to the general area where she nursed her youngster before. There she is besieged by hungry mouths. Already the clamor of baby calls has shrilled to a maximum in response to the wing rustlings and echo-locating cries of the adults as they return to the seclusion of their hideaway. Someday we may know what distinctive feature identifies each call of young and parent, getting them together in total darkness. The final decision seems to depend on scent.

Bats have developed their dependence on calls and hearing far more than any other mammals. A similar dependence on sound is shown by the few kinds of birds that nest in caves. Swiftlets in the East Indies and oilbirds in northern South America find their way, after nighttime foraging, back to their cave or hollow tree, where their young await food from the outside world. The swiftlets earn fame in human cultures by gluing together their nests with saliva rich in protein, which can be used to make "bird's-nest-soup"—a local delicacy. The oilbirds construct far cruder supports with plant fibers and droppings. They also discard onto the cave floor large numbers of palm seeds brought back as food for their young. The seeds sprout on the cave floor, nourished by other droppings from the birds, but die after using up the nourishment in each seed. Without light to provide more energy, the palm seedlings wither after growing a foot tall or more. They dry and become fibers for oilbird nests. The birds hover in flight and find the fibers by echoes from the special calls.

While all this action continues, our human ears detect only insistent clicking. The useful calls are all at wavelengths of sound too short to stimulate our hearing. A few scientists have explored this ultrasonic realm and discovered how many animals make use of it in communication, or could. The first to do so was the British experimenter Sir Francis Galton, who invented a special ultrasonic whistle with which to call his dog without disturbing anyone. A century later, pet stores sell whistles of this kind, while Galton is best remembered for his discoveries about human heredity and how fingerprints might be used for identifying people.

A dog must be rewarded for responding to a Galton whistle, even though the sound of it carries for great distances. Baby bats and the young of swiftlets and oilbirds learn how to rely on echoes of their own ultrasonic calls by accompanying their parents. The bats that pursue insects as food seem to depend on mother's milk for a longer time than those bats whose natural food will be nectar from tropical flowers. By human standards, these flying mammals learn slowly as compared to the young of mammals other than bats. The long dependency on their mothers may reflect merely the unusually long lifespan of bats, which meet few dangers in the night sky or the cave refuge—other than a storm, a crash, or unappeased hunger.

The weight that a mother bat unloads as she hangs her growing baby on the bat-roost wall before she flies off on a night mission has counterparts among mothers that walk with legs on the ground.

Many bats live almost as long as whales, showing that their lives include comparatively few hazards. They, too, have one baby at a time, usually one a year. Each bat is skillful at dodging owls as well as obstacles and meets virtually no other predators as it hunts in darkness for flying insects or ripe tropical fruits. Even when a mother bat parks her baby on the wall of the cave until she returns, rather than carrying it with her as she flies, it is in little danger of being disturbed. The secluded life of bats and their regular maternal care keep the death rate so low that the birth rate can be low, too.

Most bats live in the tropics, but they can be found on every continent except Antarctica. There is also a tremendous size range. The smallest mammal in the world is a bat the size of a bumblebee, weighing about .07 of an ounce and having a four-inch wingspan. The largest bat weighs about 2.2 pounds and has a wingspan of nearly six feet.

Bats belong to the order Chiroptera, meaning "hand wing": The skeleton of their hands supports the wing membrane, which stretches from the elongated fingers to the ankle. These mammals have been on earth for at least fifty million years. Except for the rodents, there are more species of bats in the world than any other mammal, about 850 in all. This is why its life history is so important and fascinating. Actually these animals at rest, with bright eyes and big ears, are appealing and are little understood.

In many parts of the world the bat is a sign of good luck. Egyptians hung a bat over the doorway of a home to prevent the entry of disease-carrying demons. Bat gods were important to many pre-Colombian civilizations in Central America. To the Chinese, bats are symbols of happiness and good fortune. At one time, Chinese mothers sewed jade buttons in the shape of a bat on the caps of their babies.

The diet of bats varies. Some eat nectar and pollen, some fruit, some leaves, some fish or frogs. Most North American bats dine almost solely on insects. Very few bats dine on blood. The vampire bats of Latin America are a nuisance to cattle owners, but their bites are not fatal to animals. In Trinidad we recall sleeping in a camp where vampires flew around all night but never disturbed us. The disease rabies can be carried by a sick bat and occurs in less than one half of one percent of the bats of North America.

Although bats are unable to see as well as other animals, their radar helps them find their night-flying prey and prevents them from flying headlong into trees, walls, and each other in the dark. They are important in dispersing seeds and pollinating flowers and are a part of our natural environment.

The mating of the bat is little known and described as random and promiscuous by Dr. Allen Kurta of Boston University, who has been studying bats extensively. During mating of an animal in the dark in a cave it is difficult to study what's going on. No one wishes to disturb an animal at such a time. But one can observe the birth of a bat. The feat of a little brown bat delivering her baby is awe-inspiring. She holds onto the roof with the skeletal equivalent of her thumbs, the projection at the top of her wing. She delivers the baby, catching the newborn with her feet and wings. The baby instinctively lunges for its mother. It manages to find the milk supply and nurse. Dr. Kurta is studying the composition of the mother bats' milk and recording changes as the young bats mature.

We remember one fascinating morning when we accompanied our friend Dr. O. Payne Pearson of the University of California and his enthusiastic family as they made their annual trip to check the numbers of lump-nosed bats in the attic of an old barn not many miles from the campus. The visit was timed to match the season when most births of the year had already occurred and the young bats would still be clinging to their mothers through the daylight hours. Even the commotion of catching them with a net would not part a baby from its mother. But to our amazement, it did trigger the birth of half a dozen little bats whose arrival in the world had somehow been delayed a few days. They were born in broad daylight while we watched.

Virtually every adult in the bat roost already had a numbered metal clip on its wing, and the recording went quickly, the Pearsons checking to see which ones were present and which missing since the previous census. Each new bat received its distinctive marker, odd numbers from one string of bands for males, even numbers from another string for females. Even the family relationships—which number on a baby matched which on a mother—went down in the book. And what of the three newborn ones that somehow got separated from their parents? They were hung on a piece of monk's cloth thumbtacked to the barn door, like reminders of jobs to be done. As each matching mother was examined and released, she braved the sunshine to flit quickly back and forth in front of the cloth and picked off her baby to her breast. She must have learned its ultrasonic voice in those hectic minutes while being caught and dropped into the holding cage. Not a baby was left behind.

7

Survival Strategies

For many a warm-blooded young animal, the safest way to
get meals on time is to stay where the mother or both parents
left food and will return with more. Immature hawks crouch
among other young hawks while waiting for parents to return
with food. Togetherness diminishes danger from predators. It
makes sense that a little bird should lie quietly in its parents'
nest until they come back to look after their youngster. To
crouch among other young, as many baby penguins do while
waiting for adults to bring food, may diminish danger for
each individual from an attack by hungry predators. But will
the parent find its own chick in the crèche before it starves?
Every day the baby needs half its own weight in food.
Experience shows that for the most part parents do find and
regurgitate for their chick partly digested fish and krill crustaceans, enabling their baby to grow up and repeat the practice when it has young of its own.

Parent robins returned to their young with insects some

Immature hawks crouch among other young hawks while waiting for parents to bring food. Togetherness diminishes danger from predators. (Courtesy of Ray C. Erickson, Bureau of Fisheries and wildlife)

twenty-nine times every hour for the period during which they were observed. A song thrush was documented as having delivered 10,080 larvae and insects in one month to its young—more than 336 bugs a day. This activity is repeated more than once during the year for some birds which have multiple families.

The time comes in every baby's life when it has to grow up and wait on itself. The animal kingdom has executed this transition amazingly. Though there are as many variations as there are species, the course seems to be the same. First, arouse the need to learn. Second, teach what they need to know to survive. Third, turn them away. Birds do this often, if only to increase their lifeline. When the baby birds begin to show signs of maturity, the parents bring less food, causing the need to learn flight and how to hunt. The seed-eating birds take to the task quicker than the insect eaters because seeds are easier to find. There is one bird who has a difficult time discharging its young from the nest: The wandering albatross cares for its peeper so well that the baby becomes too fat to move. The baby albatross is left alone for four months so it can reduce, and even then it must be driven from the nest.

We see the same requirements where a large number of cliff swallows have built their gourd-shaped mud nests on a rocky precipice. Each nest holds a single hungry chick who must somehow identify itself to its parents as they return with a cropful of insect prey to be shared. The hovering adults sort out the distinctive quavers of their own chick among those of perhaps two thousand others calling at once and get the food into the right mouth. Young barn swallows meet a similar need with a backup system, by wearing slightly different patterns of white markings on their heads, which the adults identify in time to locate their own youngster.

We might expect the nestling to possess the inborn ability to summon its own parents, since without them it has no future. A parent may make its own identification easier by producing distinctive calls the chick recognizes. Young laughing gulls, only six to thirteen days old, will respond to the calls of their own parent by turning toward the sound, moving conspicuously, and calling, too. Calls from nonparent laughing gulls cause the chicks to turn away, sit or crouch motionless, and make no sound. Fifteen seconds suffice for the chicks to identify their own parents and begin actions that might induce the adults to bring food.

Faithfulness is evident among other birds that must travel long distances from their chicks to find food. European white storks build rooftop nests in northern countries, often atop horizontal wagon wheels that people mount on pedestals over houses and public buildings. From these urban settings, where people provide some protection, the parent storks fly their hazardous ways to marshes and roadside pools where they can catch frogs and fish of several kinds, and sometimes a small snake. These trophies the parent bird swallows to haul home and regurgitate for the waiting young. Even a cropful of water to slake thirst is welcomed by the growing chicks.

Juvenile storks greet returning parents with a wonderful display of spread black-and-white wings and tail feathers and a cacophony of beak clapping, to which the arriving adults respond in kind before distributing their trophies. Any youngster left marooned on its nest above the city has no future if an accident befalls its parents. No other stork will come to feed it, and its display routine soon falters for lack of driving energy.

Birds of prey and those that scavenge leave their chicks in similar jeopardy. The little peregrine falcon that tends its eggs and young in some small pocket eroded from the side of a steep cliff on some American mountain, coast, or woodland, like the great California condor using as nursery a narrow ledge high on a mountain slope, follows the same tradition. So, in the Old World, do the European griffins, which lay a single egg requiring up to fifty-two days to hatch, and the great lammergeyer—largest of the kites—in mountains of southern Europe, central Asia, and Africa. The lammergeyer soars off on its narrow ten-foot wings to find bones that vultures have discarded but that will yield nutritious marrow when broken open by being dropped on rocks. Its chick whistles excitedly to the returning parents and they to it, until the cropful of hard-gleaned food can be shared.

Young gulls only a few days old will respond to the calls of their own parents by turning toward the sound and calling, too. (Courtesy of C.G. Fairchild, Bureau of Sports Fisheries and Wildlife)

One of the heaviest of all parent birds is the male mute swan, which may weigh forty pounds and still possess the power necessary to fly well. Mute-swan parents build their sturdy nests with twigs and bits of plant materials from the bottom of the nearest body of water. It may be a pond, a river, or a stream. Into that water the adult birds will lead their young the day after they hatch. New-hatched swans (cygnets) are bright-eyed and alert, able to swim and to peck at green particles of floating duckweed or tiny snails creeping over the bottom where the water is shallow. Sometimes their mother and father, who stay in close attendance, pump their big webbed feet up and down to loosen small bits of food the cygnets can swallow. Weighing only a few ounces when they emerge from the shell, the cygnets double their weight in a week. By autumn, they must have adult plumage and learn to fly with their parents. Swans need open water all winter and may travel for miles from their nesting region to find a suitable place. By early spring they are back again, repairing their nests and getting ready for another family.

These antics of mute swans are also found among swans of other continents. Mutes are native to Europe, from Poland to the marshy mouth of the Danube River in Romania. Those introduced to the British Isles are protected by tradition as "royal birds" belonging to the reigning monarch—queen or king. Black swans are native to Australia, black-necked swans to southern South America, where coscoroba swans resemble geese and seem intermediate in their growth and habits. North America has big trumpeter swans in the west and north and smaller tundra swans nesting along arctic coasts. Europe has tundra swans, too, and farther south large whooping swans with lemon-yellow beaks. All of these wonderful birds are most protective of their young and defend also the vicinity of the nest as private territory.

Birds have no need to be large to show care for their chicks

Adult swans lead their young, weighing a few ounces, into the water the day after they are hatched. The young double in weight in a week and are able to swim and peck at green particles of food. (Courtesy of Great Bend City Park, Kansas, Bureau of Sports Fisheries and Wildlife)

and bring them food. Diminutive hummingbirds show equal responsibility as they bring sticky spiderweb and bits of green lichen with which to secure a tiny nest to a tree branch. One mother hummer of the tropical kind called a Nicaraguan hermit made her nest of fibers at the tip of a downward-facing palm frond. By day she was off so much visiting flowers for nectar that her eggs seemed utterly neglected. But each night she was back to keep them warm, even tolerating a group of fascinated people with flashlamps and photoflash equipment as they set up a big camera on a sturdy tripod to take her picture. When you get to watch a mother hummer feed her chicks by regurgitating nectar, you may fear she will skewer each one to the bottom of the nest as she slides her long slender beak down the baby's throat. Any nestling hummer that fails to open wide must be sick, ready to be pulled from the nest and dropped on the ground before its illness spreads to other youngsters in the nest. The lesson is harsh but is one that every hatchling seems to understand. Weeks later the surviving young will be standing one at a time on the backs of their nestmates to have space in which to buzz their wings and prepare for flight. In another day or so, their parent may have to find the young birds perched on a limb of the same or another tree nearby, waiting for a load of nectar to be brought wherever they are. Already the fledglings know how to take off and land. Knowing how to get nectar takes a few lessons from the parents.

Each spring we marvel at a house wren that builds a nest in an empty gourd we hang on a tree just outside the study window. She scavenges among the larch branches and under the elms for twigs of a size and weight matching her kinesthetic criteria. She brings each one to the inch-wide "doorway" of the gourd and stands on the little perch provided while she nibbles her way along toward the end of the twig. Then she tries to enter the doorway with it. If it catches crosswise, she hauls it back and nibbles again toward the same or the opposite end. At least a quarter of the time, she goes too far and loses the twig to gravity. Invariably she goes in anyway—as though she had something to add to the tangle inside. Never have we seen her dive to the ground after the twig she dropped, as a chickadee will do with a seed. No more than three in every four of her tries, based on instinct and kinesthetic sense, actually contribute toward the nest.

Kinesthetic sense is a part of self-awareness we often overlook. It and memory are served by adjoining parts of the human brain—the cerebrum. Much of it, in fact, eludes any conscious investigation. If we stop to think how we manage something, we suddenly lose our hard-won ability. We are like the centipede in the story, unable to run when asked, "Which leg goes after which?"

How does a toddler, learning to balance on two feet, link slight changes in the tension of leg muscles and pressure sensors in the soles? How might we make better use of our inner senses of coordination? Surely the more we understand them, the more we are likely to benefit from further applications.

Everywhere, the bond between mother and young, whether newly hatched or born, is the strongest bond of all. In polar regions both south and north, babies of eared seals wait on a floating ice cake until mother returns with milk after she is herself well fed from a fishing expedition. The seal pup keeps alert, ready to dive into water if an arctic fox or a polar bear approaches—the seal takes its chances on climbing out again after the danger has departed. In the Antarctic the usual predator will be a large gull-like bird, such as a fulmar or a skua. A young elephant seal will wait for days at a time in warmer locations while its mother goes off to feed, leaving her pup on the beach where a huge male may accidentally roll or step on it, or some hungry bird attack. She is worth waiting for, because her milk is among the richest in the animal kingdom, supporting weight gain of her pup that averages 150 pounds in three weeks.

Flamingo birds show the strong family bond, whether newly hatched or born. (Courtesy of Lorus J. Milne and Margery Milne, Durham, New Hampshire)

Skillful Seals and Kin

The behavior of many animals adjusts to different actions that allow survival in some situations and not in others because the hazards of life vary so much from place to place. Staying put while waiting is just one way that often pays off. Even sleeping habits become specialized. The big gray seals of northern waters find secluded places to nap ashore where land predators cannot reach them. The seal simply relaxes in open water, letting itself bob up and down at the surface with only its nose out, while air in its lungs and a generous layer of fat beneath its skin combine to keep it afloat. Walruses prefer to sleep ashore in large herds on some remote beach, each animal on its back or side, with its wonderful tusks sagging close to its chest. If one walrus awakens and rolls over, the nearest neighbor must do the same, and the next, and the next. Such is the cost of a pajama party!

Often sea lions seem more versatile. On a warm, secluded shore many may snooze in close proximity. Others will roll indolently all day in the nearest fairly calm water, each raising one flipper and turning it toward the sun to capture heat and compensate for warmth lost from the body to the cool water.

Seals that migrate each year for long distances show extreme regularity in returning to give birth on the site where they themselves were born. Northern fur seals return year after year to within thirty feet of the same place, bear their single pup of the year, and, while fasting, stay with it for about six weeks until it can be weaned. Probably this is because the pup must be big and fat—as much as seven feet long and weighing nearly 150 pounds—to survive in the cold water. Feeding one large pup seems all that can be expected of one mother.

Fur-seal young are far from helpless at birth. Their eyes open seconds after being born, and their flippers flail wildly

95

before they are even out of the birth canal. Already they know how to swim if necessary. Each will live only briefly with its parent and, after being weaned, rarely stay with others of its kind from which it might learn appropriate behavior. It has more need to learn how to be a skillful hunter than to socialize, for its prey—fish and squids—are hard to find. Seals seem eager to learn and impress the observer with their intelligence. Sea lions show the same abilities with complex learning tasks, such as dolphins and apes perform. This makes them ideal subjects for exhibitions of "trained seals."

Far down on the scale of appreciated intelligence among wild animals are the manatees of warm coastal and contiguous fresh waters in the Americas and the related dugongs of the Red Sea and Eastern Hemisphere. They seem better adapted than seals to sleep concealed by water, lying on their backs on the bottom except for periodic visits to the surface to breathe in air. As these massive animals feed on underwater or waterside vegetation, each one-thousand-pound adult consumes as much as sixty to eighty pounds of plant foods daily, exposing its snout only momentarily to inhale. The female does not attain sexual maturity until she is about eight feet long, at three or four years of age. Thereafter she may bear a calf, less often two, in alternate years until accident or disease strike her down. The contribution she actually makes to the population of her kind depends on having a mate and a quiet place and her life expectancy. So far no one has discovered how long or short this is or how fast her productivity is changing as seclusion becomes ever harder to find. How could any homesick sailor have mistaken these ponderous creatures for mermaids, even though they do clasp their single young to their breasts with a clawless flipper until the young can go off alone? The fossil evidence leads many zoologists to believe that manatees, dugongs, and elephants had a common ancestor less than sixty million years ago.

Odd-toed Horse

Keeping close to Mother wherever she goes may be simpler and safer. After a mother horse (mare) carries her developing foal inside her for almost exactly one year, she lies down to give birth to it. Most of the time this occurs at night, a relic of ancient behavior that helped in survival when horses were wild: Darkness offers some safety from predators. She waits patiently for the foal to struggle to its feet. At first it stays so close to her that their shadows merge, as though the foal could cast none of its own. This may indicate merely timidity, or it could be an inborn recognition that its mother's milk awaits discovery. In just a few minutes the wobbly youngster begins searching under its mother for the two nipples between her hind legs from which it takes its first meal. So quickly does it learn where her milk awaits it that the foal will raise its nose to the correct location on a painting of a horse shown in side view, perhaps on the vertical side of the barn. Long-legged and already muscular, with senses alert, the foal needs only a few hours before it can run with the herd. With practice racing after or beside its mother, it soon can progress with other gaits, too: cantering, trotting, and galloping. Already a horse fancier will be distinguishing it as a colt if a male, or a filly if a female, and watching to see if it can outrun its mother in the games both play together. Not until the foal is three years old and weighs more than a thousand pounds will it be called a horse. With good fortune it has twenty-five to thirty years of life ahead and much more to learn during all that time. If, from the beginning, the foal gets used to a person or two who treat it kindly, it accepts them as friends and later requires no force to accustom it to pulling a load or carrying a rider on a saddle.

Wild zebras of three different kinds on the African plains follow a schedule of life much like that of the horse. Uniquely, each dominant stallion leads one or more mares and their young, each of them recognizing the others in the group by stripe pattern, voice, and scent. The group can mingle with herds of their own kind or of antelopes and then join up again with neither gain nor loss. The dominance of the stallion shows in his efficiency more in driving away his sons when they reach physiological maturity at five or six years of age than in preventing his daughters from being abducted when they reach maturity at thirteen to fourteen months. By age thirty months they usually have settled down into a lasting relationship with the stallion that starts them off on their first pregnancy. Usually a zebra mare's first pregnancy lasts 390 days, whereas when she is older she can produce a foal in as little as 345 days.

Even-toed Deer

Deer on most continents show fascinating similarities. The gestation period of the white-tailed doe is about two hundred days, with the fawns conceived in November and born in late May or early June. When the time comes for the doe to give birth, she generally seeks solitude. Young does (one to two years old) usually have a single birth. Older does in good condition generally bear twins or even triplets. The entire birth is rapid and almost bloodless and takes less than thirty seconds. The mother doe licks her newborn fawn all over and learns its identifiable scent during the first six minutes after it is born. By the seventh minute the fawn has recovered from the shock of being in air and may start nursing anywhere up to two hours. Following its first meal, the doe begins teaching her baby the facets of fear, for fear is the deer's main defense. To survive, the fawn must hide or run from a vast array of dangers, often merely when it hears a bird sound an alarm. The doe will remain with its fawn(s) during nighttime, and it will browse during daylight, returning often to nurse her young. A young fawn's coat has approximately three hundred white spots, giving it good camouflage for its protection. Fawns nurse heavily for two months and will be weaned at three and one half months.

The "red deer" so familiar to Europeans is the antlered equivalent of the American elk. An adult male is a *stag*, a female a *hind*, their baby a *calf* that shows few special features until later. In rutting season the stags roar their challenges to others of their kind and mostly space themselves apart rather than do actual battle for dominance. Only about one in twenty stags gets permanently injured by fights for control of a harem of hinds. Curiously, the young born from matings of dominant stags and their dominant hinds turn out to be preponderantly male calves, whereas subordinate stags with subordinate hinds yield far more female calves. Male calves get nursed oftener and for longer than female calves but use up their nourishment in faster growth. This puts them at a later disadvantage. Large, dominant hinds displace smaller hinds from the richest food resources and continue as the most effective breeders. Excellent nourishment gives their calves a distinct advantage toward faster growth and more vigorous maturity. Only at the moment of giving birth do all the hinds appear equal, each busy licking to cleanse the newborn, then standing to nurse it within minutes after giving birth.

Europeans use the name *elk* for the kind of antlered animal known in North America as a moose. Thousands of these creatures roam swamplands of northern states and Canada. Largest are those in Alaska, where from low flying aircraft six white moose have been located. One of the six is a magnificent bull with huge antlers, still in his prime after repelling packs of hungry wolves that search for any moose with a handicap. Whether this variant from the normal dark brown color is a heredity relic from something common during the Ice Age thousands of years ago is unclear. Not one of the white animals is an albino, and white could be the future color—an adaptive advantage in country that is often snow-covered for many months each year.

Biggest Land Animal

A few kinds of animals grow so bulky and heavy that the baby can take shelter under its mother. The biggest animals on land—the African elephants—carry their babies for as long as 660 days before birth and bear just one at a time. Yet by comparison with a newborn whale, the newborn elephant is small—rarely more than three hundred pounds and only three feet tall. When standing up as high as possible, it can barely reach its mother's milk. Nor is there any use in waiting for her to lie down: She sleeps on her feet. To relax the muscles that support her heavy head, she just rests one tusk on a low branch of a tree and drapes her trunk comfortably over that tusk. The cow elephant has only to keep her newborn baby between her massive legs to fend off any predator. Whenever she stands for an extended period, the young elephant may lie on its side, perhaps with one gigantic ear folded forward to shield its exposed eye. It seems to need a lot of sleep. When the mother is about to move on, she will help her youngster to its feet. Letting the baby elephant lag behind or stray even a few yards from her increases the risk that it will be killed.

In his *Origin of Species* the great naturalist Charles Darwin noted:

> The elephant is reckoned the slowest breeder of all
> known animals and I have taken some pains to esti-
> mate its probable minimum rate of natural increase:

100

it will be under the mark to assume that it breeds when thirty years old, and goes on breeding till ninety years old, bringing forth three pair of young in this interval; if this be so, at the end of the fifth century there would be alive fifteen million elephants descended from the first pair.

At the Bronx Zoo in 1981 officials tried to weigh a baby elephant born at the zoo in August. When the recalcitrant pachyderm refused to step onto the scale, she was weighed together with her mother (5,396 pounds). The mother was then weighed alone (5,033 pounds), allowing the baby's weight to be calculated (363 pounds).

Less than two weeks after it is born, the little elephant begins to show its first teeth. They are heavy grinders, one above and one below on each side of its mouth. But it does not begin to use them or to wean itself until it is three months old.

During its entire lifetime, an elephant grows only six grinding teeth on each side of its jaw. It follows a strange schedule that lets it have only one tooth in service above and below on each side of its mouth most of the time. Fortunately, the grinders are large and crush effectively the hard vegetation the elephant eats.

The young elephant gets its second set of grinders late in its second year of life. Soon after they are in service, the grinders of the first set drop out. A third set of grinders comes into use at age five. A few months later, the second set drops out, leaving the third grinders to serve the elephant until it is nine years old.

A fourth set of grinders begins to show while the animal is six years old but takes almost three years to grow into position for use. These are regarded as the first of the elephant's adult

Young African elephants can take shelter under their mother. Weighing three hundred pounds, babies stand three feet tall and can barely reach the mother's milk. (Courtesy of Satour, South Africa Tourist Corporation)

teeth. Generally they become noticeable at the same time as its tusks, which are strangely shaped incisor teeth on its upper jaw.

Apparently the tusks keep on growing as long as an elephant is well nourished. The record pair from an African elephant are ten feet, two and a half inches long and together weigh 226 1/2 pounds.

In the human pattern of reproduction, babies are born every week throughout the year. But most other animals have only a single season of births. Ordinarily the inherited pattern calls for births in a month when the parents can find food easily. It is followed by a time of year when the things the young can eat are as abundant as possible. This explains why so many young animals are born at the beginning of spring and are weaned by early summer while plants are still growing vigorously.

Largest Sea Mammal

The largest animals of all—the great blue whales, which grow to be more than a hundred feet long—follow a strict, inherited schedule of this kind. Their program matches their migration habits. These are tied to the annual changes in the abundance of food for whales in the oceans north and south of the equator. While winter spreads over the northern hemisphere, the whales are swimming near the coast of Antarctica. At that time of year the days are long there and the weather as warm as it ever gets. Benefiting from the sunlight, minute plants that drift in the ocean water multiply prodigiously. Small fish and inch-long shrimplike crustaceans called *krill* devour the plants and reproduce at top speed. The whales filter the small fish and krill from the water and swallow them. This diet is extremely nourishing to a whale. Indeed, it gains weight so rapidly that by March it is fat enough to fast for weeks while it swims north through tropical waters into the northern Pacific Ocean. By the time winter comes to the southern hemisphere and the long days of summer arrive in northern oceans, the whales are there, feeding on the krill and small fish that now are growing rapidly in the north.

In April, when the great blue whales are swimming north through the warm waters of the tropics, the young blue whales are born. Twins are rare. Usually a mother whale gives birth to a single youngster, which is about twenty-three feet long and already weighs about fourteen thousand pounds. It swims immediately, keeping close to its mother. From time to time she rolls over onto her side to let the big baby nurse. With special muscles she helps transfer her milk, squirting it down the youngster's throat without much need for suction. For a year or more she feeds it in this way. Her milk is so rich that the young whale grows at an amazing pace. By the time it is weaned, it may be fifty-six feet long and weigh fifty tons. At three years of age it can find a mate and begin reproduction, although the young whale will continue to increase in size until it is at least twelve years old.

Since a mother great blue whale carries her baby inside her for almost a year before it is born and nurses it so generously for another twelve to fourteen months afterward, she gives birth only once every two or three years. Each baby is born at a time when it will encounter the warmest water possible. There it can get used to swimming before it reaches the chilly parts of the northern Pacific Ocean. It will first follow its mother far north, then back down to Antarctic waters, and finally north again before she weans it. By that time it will be able to filter food from the oceans so efficiently that it, too, can fast while swimming through the tropics, where suitable nourishment is scarce.

As another example of the survival patterns of the baby world, whole herds of Cape buffalo in Africa, like musk-oxen in the far north, react to danger by standing in a circle around their babies, with horned heads outward and all young of the group safely at the center of the ring. Getting a tender young-ster to eat becomes too dangerous for a predator to attempt, not worth the risk of being hurt by the vigilant parents.

Human Development

Most human babies continue to grow for a full forty weeks inside their mother. A few wait until the forty-fourth week before being born. During these extra weeks, the body of the baby gains fat deposits that round out its contours. Its nervous system gives it new capabilities. It can respond more quickly to the spectrum of sounds, lights, tastes, smells, contacts, and changes in temperature that await it in the world outside its mother.

Some systems that the fetus develops during the first twenty-eight weeks are as perfect as they will ever be. They can be called upon and must not fail whenever the fetus is born, whether it is during the twenty-eighth week or not until the forty-fourth week of development. No one knows yet how much advance warning the fetus that is about to be born gets. Certainly it has no choice. The muscles that surround the baby in its mother's womb suddenly contract and then relax again. Perhaps a half hour later, the next spasm of contraction comes. Gradually the intervals between one contraction and the next get shorter, and the vigor of the muscular effort increases. Only one route is available for the fetus: out through its mother's birth canal. The passageway widens in preparation. The "bag of water" that surrounded the fetus like a private aquarium bursts and lubricates the birth canal. Strong contractions urge the baby onward, out of its warm, wet place of security into a drafty, dry, dangerous world.

For a few moments after slipping out, the human baby is still tethered by its umbilical cord to the placenta inside its mother's womb. But the cord is soon cut and tied. Once it is discarded, the baby's blood can no longer flow that way. Instead, the blood must go past the lungs and be ventilated there as the baby breathes in and out. Breathing requires muscular work and is an activity the baby has never tried before. Yet it must continue pumping in air and exhaling it again to stay alive. No future change in the baby's way of life will ever be so drastic.

For a few days after being born, each infant loses weight.

Some of the loss is just water, but the baby needs time, too, to get used to swallowing food, carrying on the processes of digestion, and attending to its own wastes. All of these activities require far more effort than merely absorbing oxygen and nourishment that the mother has already taken into her blood stream.

Most infants adjust well to their new routine. Actually, they have already completed most of their growth by the day of birth. At an average weight of seven and a half pounds, the full-term baby is nearly two billion times heavier than the fertilized egg from which it grew in just nine months. Within the next year, it will still be average if it grows to weigh twenty-two pounds. After that it can never again triple its weight in so short a time without danger of becoming too fat. At twenty times its birth weight, the body reaches essentially full size. During the last part of the inherited schedule, growth gradually slows down, and finally it stops at about twenty years of age.

Frogs and Tadpoles

The changes within our lifetime involve the obsolescence—often the death and destruction—of whole organs, without affecting normal development as a whole. They differ little from the alterations that transform a tadpole into a frog, destroying the cells of gills and tail while its lungs and legs are growing. They mirror our quick adjustment while moving from an aquatic existence to an aerial life at birth.

For a frog to offer parental care to tadpole offspring seems even more remarkable. When a tadpole changes its body form to become a frog or a toad, it ordinarily loses weight. So does a caterpillar as it transforms into a moth or a butterfly. Part of this loss is due to the enforced fasting during the changeover.

The rest of the loss is brought about by destruction of cells in altering the body form. Although the animal is growing up, it shrinks by a process called *negative growth*. Ironically, this customary change has led to a misinterpretation in local lore as it relates to a smooth-skinned green amphibian of marshes and swamps in Trinidad and northern South America. People there have named the amphibian the paradox frog *(Pseudis paradoxa)*, believing it to transform itself from a three-inch adult into a ten-inch tadpole, paradoxically growing younger and heavier, rather than older and much lighter. The monstrous tadpole does weigh several times as much as the adult paradox frog. But in captivity, the spectacular negative growth of the tadpole can be seen taking place during transformation into the small adult.

The stage in which an animal is born and the particular pattern of growth it follows are clearly related to the environment from which its nourishment must come. The mother must have adequate food, and the young must mature into a world where they can find their own food.

Should it not be enough that the parent frog hunts out in spring the pond or stream that will be a suitable habitat for these swimming young after they hatch from the jelly-coated eggs she lays? The spring peeper goes to a narrow brook just as it frees itself of winter ice, the woodfrog to a woodland pond later in the spring, and the big bullfrog to a lake edge in early summer, when food for its tadpoles will be available for the two years or longer of their aquatic stage, before they grow legs and come ashore. But the arrow-poison frogs of tropical America do more. They hunt out little puddles of water held by the leaf bases of plants perching on high limbs in the rain forest as sites for their few eggs, then return weeks later to let the growing tadpoles climb on their mother's back and hold on there while she hunts out a bigger lofty puddle in which her tadpoles can continue their growth. If the original small puddle holds more than one of her young, she makes several trips, as though patterning her behavior after that of a cat moving her kittens one at a time to greater safety.

Every living baby grows according to its own distinctive schedule. From the very beginning it follows a complex program of enlargement, change, and repair.

A scattering of other creatures have developed the habit of remaining while young where their mother will both protect them and also provide nourishment. The tropical discus fish of Amazon fresh waters secretes from the side of its body a jelly rich in proteins, which the hatchlings eat. Their behavior reminds us that the milk produced by all mother mammals comes from special skin glands embedded beneath the surface. None of the amphibians or reptiles possess this feature, which leaves their young hungry even if the mother guards them until they hatch and go off on their own.

Invertebrates

Among animals that lack a backbone (the invertebrates), an utterly different system may be followed to keep the young protected and fed in some kind of nest. This system satisfies the needs of all the social species (termites, ants, bees, and some wasps). From their nest the adults go forth for more food, then return to share it with the hatchlings. Not until the young reach maturity will they build nests and forage for nourishment, although while immature they may share in the tasks of distributing food to still younger individuals in the colony.

Much less conspicuously, some mother scorpions living in tropical Africa retain their eggs until they hatch and then provide food internally for the hatchlings while they are still in her body. It is as though the mother scorpion has inside her a

Certain horned lizards give birth to a miniature copy of the parent. A youngster may clamber onto the mother piggyback as she moves along. The family has a chance to catch insects for food. (Courtesy of Lorus J. Milne and Margery Milne, Durham, New Hampshire)

bottle with a nipple to convey food right into her baby's mouth. Some other scorpions lay their eggs in crevices or little depressions in the earth and may hover over them until they hatch. The young may then climb on the mother's back and ride along wherever she goes, getting some practice at intervals in dashing off, catching and swallowing some small insect as prey, and hurrying back aboard.

We observed a common horned lizard in the American Southwest carry its young in a similar way. After giving birth to miniature copies of herself, one or more of the babies happen to clamber onto her piggyback, and she moves along. The lucky travelers hitch a ride on their mother's back to hunting places they could scarcely reach by walking or running on their own. This gives them more chance to find insects small enough to catch and eat. Meanwhile, their mother detects larger insects for herself and stays well fed.

In the American Southwest and Mexico, complicated spider webs extend between the telephone wires strung from pole to pole. Many spiders of a single kind cooperate in producing these webs and feed on whatever middle-sized or large flying insects they catch. Theirs is an integrated community in which hatchling spiders are welcome to take as food the really small insects that get caught—victims too small to interest the adult spiders. By staying in the communal nest, the youngsters get food and some protection without having to be fed by their own parents. The effect is the same, even though the method is so different.

8

Marsupials and Reptiles

For a newborn opossum or kangaroo, the only hospitable site in all the world awaits it inside its mother's pouch. There she has milk to offer. Getting there and starting to nurse can be a major ordeal. Success is far from guaranteed, even though the pregnant mother sits down firmly and uses her tongue to wet her fur along the route the newborn must take to reach her pouch. The baby generally has a pear-shaped body and strong front legs but not yet any hind legs or tail. Hooking its claws into her wet fur, it lets gravity determine its aim like a pendulum as it hauls itself upslope to the rim of her pouch, falls in, and seeks a nipple. Usually the number of nipples is less than the number of babies. Latecomers find no teat waiting for them because every one has been claimed by an earlier arrival. Soon the end of each nipple expands within the baby's stomach, like a button that prevents it from being slid out again until the youngster grows a lot. No wonder the Dutch explorer and merchant Francisco Pelsaert claimed in 1629, on the basis of his examination of the young in a kangaroo's pouch, that the baby grew from the teat in a unique kind of sexless reproduction! A newborn baby with no nipple has no future, either.

From watching a litter of newborn pigs, you could easily conclude that all firstborns have a distinct advantage. With two to fourteen piglets in a litter and no more than six pairs of nipples, sometimes fewer, those born last may find every source of milk already taken. Those newborn that manage to get a good meal become violently determined to maintain access to the supply—developing a hierarchy among those vigorous enough to fight for a place. Soon each individual claims a particular nipple.

A mother kangaroo has only two nipples to offer. Her most recent baby gets one and attaches itself firmly to receive a very rich milk. Her previous youngster—one that has grown too big to re-enter her pouch—still depends on getting a meal from her on frequent visits. It is her "foot baby," which stays close by and never disturbs her newest young while getting its share of milk from her second nipple, which produces a less nutritious milk. If the mother kangaroo has to race away from some obvious danger, even her newest baby may not be safe. To save herself she may abandon her foot baby, then dislodge and discard the young in her pouch. For a red kangaroo, all is not lost. If the mother escapes, she finds safety somewhere with no baby using either nipple. Ordinarily she has another embryo ready to be born in a few days. It has been waiting since last she mated, like a "spare part" to serve after an emergency. As soon as it is born and safely in her pouch, she is ready to mate again.

These unfamiliar actions by pouched mothers—marsupials—astonished the scientists who discovered them. Europe and Asia have no native marsupials, and North America acquired its opossums from South America, where a few inconspicuous marsupials still live.

Each marsupial baby kangaroo sticks its head out of its mother's pouch and samples the vegetation on which she is feeding, thereby developing the ability to discriminate the familiar from the unfamiliar. (Courtesy of Australia Tourist Agency)

At latitudes from Washington, D.C., north into southern Canada, opossums have only one litter each year, but they start early. In February, males begin looking for females as well as food and for a short time pair off, forsaking their natural solitary habits. A female that is only a year old and inexperienced in sex may resent the approach of any male and continually snap at him. Her lips draw back to expose her sharp teeth. She chatters them and growls at him. Since he is smaller than she, he does well to heed her warning. He seems to count on her eventual acceptance of his services. When she does let him mount, he is quick about it and soon hurries off. Her pregnancy lasts twelve and a half days. During the last week, she gathers fresh, dry bedding into her den. With her pointed jaws, she arranges plant fibers into a wad and pushes them below her abdomen. In this position she can support the wad by curling her naked, scaly, prehensile tail between her legs like a long, slender finger. Holding the bedding firmly, she ambles along to her shelter.

The actual birth takes less than an hour, during which the mother lies back with her tail extended. One after another, the tiny young emerge from her birth canal. Each is about the size of a honeybee and so bare that some of its internal organs can be seen through its translucent skin. Yet it uses gravity to aim its course as it uses its forelegs to haul itself through the tangled curls on its mother's belly to the opening of her pouch. As many as eighteen start off this obstacle race, with no more than thirteen nipples waiting for the winners. Any babies that miss the pouch or get there after the "restaurant" is full keep on crawling until they die. The successful ones must cope with accidents. Fewer than ten usually survive for the month before they first peek out of her pouch.

At five weeks, baby opossums try emerging altogether. At eight weeks, they are weaned and may go off on their own. After twelve weeks, their mother gives them no choice about leaving her. In the southern United States she may be getting ready for her next mating. In Latin America this frequently produces the second of three litters in succession.

Readiness to eat a wide range of foods, fresh or not, makes nourishment no real problem for opossums throughout their range, which extends through South America as far as Argentina. But already these versatile marsupials have reached their northward limit. Across Michigan the boundary coincides with a climatic line beyond which winter weather confines opossums for more than seventy days between autumn and spring. No matter how soundly the opossums sleep when the cold and snow prevent them from foraging, their store of fat cannot last longer than this. They may go through the routine of mating in February, then starve to death before their young have had a chance to see the world.

Australia, but not New Zealand, has been abundantly supplied with marsupial mammals. In the big down-under continent they had so many different habitats available that marsupials diversified into the meat-eating Tasmanian "wolf" and "devil," marsupial "rats," brush-tailed "mice," and others resembling tree shrews, moles, flying squirrels (sugar gliders), cats, banded anteaters, or the unique bandicoots, koalas, cuscuses, wombats, tree kangaroos, wallabies, and plain kangaroos. Some of them keep their young in a pouch only for a while, then carry their babies about attached firmly to nipples in the open until the burdens get excessive.

Each kind of youngster has its own problems to meet as soon as it is free from its mother. For a young koala, it may be to find another eucalyptus tree of the correct kind where it can feed on foliage without competing with its mother. A young Tasmanian devil must catch enough small animals for food without most escaping and find a hiding place for each day in which to rest until night brings hunting time again.

Each marsupial baby may develop important habits before

it goes off on its own. The young kangaroo sticks its head out of its mother's pouch and samples the vegetation on which she is feeding. In this way it develops the ability to discriminate between the familiar and unfamiliar and avoids the latter as unsuitable, even if safe and nourishing. The koala's pouch, concealing two nipples, opens at the rear instead of at the front. This protects the young koala, weighing at birth no more than three quarters of a pound, while its mother hangs by her hind legs and feeds suspended in a tree. The youngster has no chance to reach from her pouch the few special kinds of eucalyptus she eats. It must become familiar with remains of distinctive odors that remain in her wastes as they are discharged near her baby. Perhaps only four are sufficiently peculiar to recall, for that is the number of eucalyptus species out of more than six hundred that a koala at any age will eat without moving away—on to another tree that might be better. Once weaned at seven inches long and age twelve months, it is a "gum baby." By age four years it can be fully grown and sexually mature, with another sixteen years to live.

A wombat, tunneling like a mole through the earth, shows few preferences among the insects, worms, and other creatures it accepts as prey. The young wombat in its parents' burrow may learn not to expose itself to the light of day and to predators (mostly birds and reptiles), but its diet seems identical to that of its parents.

Parental Reptiles

Just occasionally the young of an animal are limited to quite different foods from those the parents eat. The mother alligator or crocodile acts as though she were warm-blooded and solicitous toward her young. She stays near her nest until she can hear them scrambling about inside the mass of mud and rotting vegetation. She may help them escape and stay close to guard them from large herons and other crocodilians. But the hatchling alligator or crocodile must satisfy its hunger by eating insects in its pond, stream, or bayou. Not until it grows a few inches longer and gets stronger can it snap at and swallow small fishes it finds along the bottom. Larger prey comes later with still more growth.

Many reptiles differ in sexual development according to the temperature. Alligator eggs incubated below 86ºF all hatch as females. Above 93ºF they hatch as males. Seemingly the cooler temperatures favor growth to larger size before hatching and attainment of maturity for breeding at an earlier age. This favors production of large numbers of young year after year.

Possibly the same rules apply to the strange mugger crocodiles that scavenge for meat in the multiple mouths of the Kaveri River near Madras in India. Twice a year the female muggers build nests but depart as soon as their eggs are laid and covered with rotting, warmth-producing vegetation. The male stays close through two to five months of incubation and, with his powerful jaws, helps the hatchlings escape or transfers the eggs to a safer location. During her lifetime a female mugger may produce three hundred eggs. Her mate improves the possibility that many will yield young muggers.

Loggerhead turtles develop in an inverse relationship to temperature, with cool eggs producing males. The American snapping turtle is stranger, in that either a low or a high temperature favors development of females, and moderate warmth in the nest leads to production of males. In any creature, the actual sex of the individual calls forth special inherited behavior without the individual knowing exactly how.

When you stop to think of reptile babies, you realize that the giants among them occurred back in the age of dinosaurs. Bringing up a pig-sized baby must have been a challenge for a twenty-five ton brontosaur mother. Babies were born alive, according to Robert T. Bakker of the University of Colorado, and they were warm-blooded. The theory is that these babies were taken care of by their mothers instead of being left to fend for themselves as most living reptiles do. The brontosaur baby weighed as much as three hundred pounds at birth and was able to emerge through the birth canal because the fossil pelvic cavity is one you could "drive a Volkswagen bug through." There was a long gestation period with the birth of a single baby rather than a large brood.

With smaller egg-laying dinosaurs, large broods occurred, according to paleontologist Jack Horner of The Museum of the Rockies in Bozeman, Montana. He explored and found entire rookeries of baby dinosaurs in what he named "Egg Mountain" in the Montana prairies. His research of many years' duration shows nests complete with numerous eggs of the duckbill dinosaur. The discoveries of fifteen baby skeletons, as well as the first of dinosaur nestlings, enabled an understanding of the young dinosaurs from egg to maturity. The theory is that the two-ton mother laid about twenty eggs at a time and kept them warm with a covering of leaves. She perhaps fed the young with available fruits and greenery, for these creatures seem to have been vegetarians. Some were ten feet long; others, like the so-called Hadrosaurs, were thirty feet from nose to tail. The nests were three feet wide and six feet deep. Some nests scooped out of the mud showed clutches of as many as twenty-five eggs tidily arranged; others showed skeletons of juveniles and the start of a family life. These dinosaurs nested in great colonies like penguins and perhaps provided early parental care. The little dinosaurs were only thirteen inches long at birth and then grew to their huge size. Horner writes: "If you're born little and have a long ways to grow, it is selectively advantageous to grow fast—and to do that you have to be warm blooded." More dinosaur family secrets are yet to be revealed as research continues.

In comparison to the dinosaur, the mother python is a mere thirty feet long. She is not warm blooded but does generate extra heat through muscle contractions and shares it by coiling around her thirty to forty eggs. She fasts throughout their slow development and remains close to the hatchlings for a week or two, until they begin to seek food on their own. They, too, can manage only prey quite unlike hers, for years must pass before they are big enough to coil around a victim and squeeze it each time it exhales. It suffocates, unable to inhale another breath. Inert, it offers no resistance to being swallowed.

Nonconstrictor snakes include several different kinds that retain their eggs inside the mother's body until the young hatch and find their way to the outside world. This type of parental care relieves the reptile from any need to build a nest and lets whatever size and fangs she has repel attackers until the last.

Garter snakes lie motionless on the floor of their den from fall through winter. With spring the temperature of the bare earth on which the snakes lie remains in the low sixty degrees Fahrenheit. After their long hibernation, the denning reptiles use up most of their stored fat. Their lidless eyes see nothing in the darkness underground. Only their own musky scent fills the air of their hiding place. But with spring, new odors act like an alarm clock.

The snakes raise their heads, flick out their tongues, breathe faster, and grow alert. Snakes react to the slight increase in temperature. Their muscles contract slightly and produce more heat. Snakes at the center of the communal tangle respond to the change in temperature by gliding slowly to the outside. As soon as they reach the cool earth, they chill into immobility again. Only the big female keeps going. She reaches the entrance and pushes through it into the sunshine. Her black tongue with its red forked tips probes into the spring air, bringing its odors back to the roof of her mouth. There she has special pits in which her sense of smell is keenest. One of the snakes in the den is a vigorous female. She is in no hurry. She has given birth to twenty-three young the year before and is pregnant once more, without having another mate. Garter snakes have the strange ability to bear litters two or three years in a row after a single mating. Now the twenty-seven unborn snakes within her body are almost five inches long. They have another inch to grow before being ready to face the world. By then their mother is definitely out of the hibernating den and finds a few small animals to eat.

The pregnant snake moves hesitantly. She glides silently. The convex scales that covered her eyes are not as transparent as they used to be. Soon she sheds them, along with the tissue-thin skin that covered her body. Her colors will be brighter and she'll see more clearly. Yet she recognizes the world outside her den. She catches and eats a beetle without moving much. An occasional meal is all she needs while she waits for her young to complete their growth inside her body to be born alive. Most of the eleven years since she was born have been spent waiting. Almost half of all that time went into waiting for winter to follow autumn and give way to spring. She must spend many hours outside the hibernation den for her body to warm up and give birth to her youngsters. The only tricky part of living longer is knowing when to wait and when to slither away as fast as she can go.

9

Nature versus Nurture

It may seem unreasonable that both in a pair of feathered parents should desert their chick while it is still hungry and receptive, particularly after these parents have diligently searched for or dug a special nest site for one or two eggs each year, then flown shuttle service with food for their hatchling. Yet many a seabird regularly follows this program: puffins and petrels, murres and auks, and shearwaters (known as muttonbirds) in the Southern Hemisphere. Admittedly they stuff their youngster with regurgitated fish until it is obese, bulging almost like a ball of fat. After its parents abandon it, the baby bird is on its own to follow its inherited guidance. As it slims down on a starvation diet, it emerges from its nest burrow on dark nights to practice using its wing muscles. It finds its way to the sea, even down murderously steep slopes, learns to swim, to catch fish whenever hungry, and to fly from wave to wave. Eventually it returns to the same shore near which it hatched, to repeat the action.

When you try to discover early enough the hole through which a young petrel will emerge on its own and wait silently beside it after night has spread, you are likely to hear the sweet song of a parent petrel returning with food. The flier calls to its mate in the nest and hears a reply before alighting at the hole and entering to feed the young and relieve the mate. Now the bird that has been incubating the egg or keeping the chick warm is free to fly off over the dark ocean and catch fish: fish for its own needs and a cropful more to bring back to the nest for the young inside.

If you find a young shearwater after it has survived being abandoned, you may follow it to the nearest seashore and watch it fly away. From New Zealand, Australia, or some island in the South Pacific, the young bird is likely to fly north. Without guidance it is prepared to circuit the Pacific Ocean before returning to its birthplace many years later—now a mature bird ready to find a mate and repeat its ancestral pattern in raising a family. Still more marvelous is the regularity with which adults and newly matured individuals arrive at their nesting destination after so many months of separate wandering—on the same night or the one before or just after. Thousands and thousands succeed in this enterprise, which has ensured survival of their species for many millennia.

A significant difference exists between the head of a bird and that of a mammal, which accounts in part for the unlike development of their sensory facilities. Most birds are active by day, depend strongly on vision, and respond little to odors. In permitting large eyes for better vision, the front region of the brain (with its sensitivity to smell) has been cramped. Instead, the rear area—where instinctive actions have their seat—has developed in extreme. Mammals, few of which fly, can be less streamlined, their heads large enough for both eyes and brain. And the smaller ones, with a weight comparable to

A whooping-crane chick is active by day and depends strongly on vision in its remarkable travels later on as an adult. (Courtesy of Luther C. Goldmon, Bureau of Sports Fisheries and Wildlife)

that of birds, are more frequently nocturnal—with less need for eyes. In consequence the cerebrum has had space to spread, and emphasis has been placed more on smell, with development of brain areas concerned with intelligence and learning. This greater ability to learn is evident even to amateur observers. A bird builds approximately as good a nest the first time as the last and shows the same excitement on each occasion that the eggs are laid or the young have hatched. In contrast, a mammal is clumsy and inept, even likely to be negligent and intolerant of her first litter. Motherhood comes harder, but the second pregnancy is handled more skillfully. She plays with the babies more and appears to enjoy their antics. At feeding time she is more willing to let them nurse. Even orphans of other families or other kinds may be adopted by an experienced mother. Instinct and learning are evident in the nursing mammal.

Distinguishing what a small wild animal gains only through the learning process and how much of its behavior is inherited may require long observation or experiments indoors. At the Max Planck Institute near Munich, newborn squirrels were kept on a liquid diet for months, with never a chance to find a nut or bare ground beyond the cement floor of their cage. When released into the outdoor world and given nuts beyond those they chose to eat, each young squirrel picked up a nut in its paws, hunted for a soft place in which to dig a hole, buried the nut, and used its forefeet to tamp down the earth over it. As the experimenter concluded, "The entire behavior sequence is preprogrammed."

The squirrel may bury dozens of nuts in different places without remembering where more than a few of them are concealed. Later, when hungry, it searches for nuts that it or some other squirrel has buried and finds quite a number in seasons when other food is scarce. Those that are missed may sprout and produce new oak trees. Probably most oaks in America were "planted" by squirrels following these inherited patterns of behavior.

Quite a different style is followed by the young of certain western woodpeckers as they learn the ways of their parents in the open colony. Many of these birds busy themselves with pecking pits in the bark of Douglas firs and other trees, while other woodpeckers of the same kind bring individual acorns and hammer them vigorously into the pits. This procedure stocks a great many trees with food, as a reserve to be drawn upon when the next brood of young hatch in the nests, needing nourishment with a minimum of time taken in locating it or bringing it home.

Occasionally we are given an unplanned demonstration of what behavior young birds have inherited, despite the teaching that an adult offers. If a broody hen is given duck eggs to incubate, she leads the hatchlings to places in which she can peck at and pick up seeds to eat. Ducklings do not imitate this activity and ignore the obvious distress of the hen if they can get to a shallow pond, swim out, and seek food from the bottom. The hen rushes back and forth, squawking, trying in the only ways she knows to bring the ducklings back to land, to seeds, away from the wet foods for which they dabble so automatically.

Also inborn is the behavior of goslings to follow a hen or a mother duck if it is the first large object they see move after they hatch into an unfamiliar world. A person can serve equally well as a surrogate parent, as can a football suspended from a horizontal clothesline and pulled above the hatchlings on their first day out of the shell. This automatic attraction, which normally pays off, is known as *imprinting*.

Even the sounds a young bird makes may follow an inherited pattern. As European naturalists discovered from observing their native graylag geese, a recently hatched gosling chirps *wee-wee* at intervals while under its mother. She responds each time. If she goes away from the nest, the *wee-wee* calls grow more insistent and frequent as distress signals. They subside when she returns and responds to the gosling.

If a songbird chick hatches in the nest of a foster parent of a different kind, the youngster begins its own style of song as soon as it is old enough to sing. If its foster parents are from a remote part of the country, far from where its own parents matured, they may use a dialect of the appropriate song. The youngster may accommodate to this, much as a child will pick up the phraseology and words of a person from Australia, Cockney London, Ontario, Canada, or the Deep South or Far West. Learning a Chinese dialect or some tribal language on an island in the Southwest Pacific is just as easy when begun soon after birth but increasingly difficult as the person becomes distracted with activities of adolescence and adult life.

Anyone with a good ear for music can recognize the difference between the song produced by a very young meadowlark and that of a mature bird. Quavers and interruptions disappear as the youngster learns through practice to duplicate the meadowlark song of its elders, but only if it can hear them singing and adjust its inherited pattern of song to theirs. In a way this improvement resembles the effects of teaching a child, providing it with an education.

Birds offer the curious scientist a wonderful opportunity to learn whether unhatched chicks might be learning more than the sound of the voices of the incubating parents. While the chick is still in the intact shell, it might also be hearing sounds from adjacent unhatched chicks. Research psychologist Margaret Vince of Cambridge University recorded faint clicks of unknown origin from quail chicks during the last three days of incubation before their expected date for hatching. So long as the egg shells were in contact to aid the sound vibrations in passing from egg to egg, the messages from more advanced chicks stimulated less developed ones to speed up and to hatch within hours of the rest. The little birds still conceal how this is done, but the near synchrony they achieve is no longer so mysterious.

Far to the north, near Edmonton, Alberta, Canadian biologist William Rowan wondered how much young crows knew about travel as hatchlings—before going anywhere. He penned up fifty-four young crows where they could neither see nor hear adults of their kind. On November 9, a whole month after the free-flying adult crows had all gone south, he released the fifty-four tagged juveniles. Around them were only snow-covered plains at a temperature below zero on the Fahrenheit scale. Off they flew. But by November 20, Rowan and his collaborators had found more than half of the young crows again. One had traveled 250 miles from the release point near Edmonton. Every one of them was found along a narrow route between there and central Oklahoma, which is the wintering ground for almost every Alberta crow. Young crows knew a lot on their own.

Such remarkable travels of birds occurred in our town with swans that we brought from Rhode Island. In the fall we drove the young birds north in our enclosed car to New Hampshire. After a two-hundred-mile trip, we introduced them to the town Mill Pond, where they met two older swans already settled in. The immature swans were not welcomed by the resident birds, but they managed nonetheless. When a winter storm blew in, they disappeared. We searched and could not locate them. Then came a message in the spring from the division of Fish and Wildlife in Rhode Island that our banded birds were found on the highway, having hit tension wires near where we had picked them up. How did the young swans know the route back to their home? They had never traveled on their own to New Hampshire. Yet they found their way to their birthplace—the place where they had started out as baby swans (cygnets).

Enterprising Beaver

The hard-working beavers of North America and Europe depend on similar enterprise by their young. Each mated pair maintains a beaver pond by building a strong dam across some running river and constructing from felled tree trunks and mud a snug lodge with an underwater entrance and surrounding moat (the pond). Very early in springtime the mother gives birth to two to eight kits within the insulated chamber of the lodge and nurses them regularly until the outside weather warms enough for fresh food to start growing. By then the pond will be free of ice, and the mother beaver can find food easily. Back to the lodge to nurse her young, out into the pond at night to get more food or to repair the dam, she gets scant rest even when her mate gives all the help he can.

Not until autumn will the mother beaver lead her kits out of the lodge to learn how to get food for themselves. Back to the lodge they go where some safety seems assured. They stay there every day until they are almost two years old. Their welcome and that of the male parent will be interrupted briefly in early spring when the mother insists on privacy while she gives birth to another litter of young. Afterward she will deny return to any babies two years old or more. They must be on their own, banished even from the parental beaver pond. Their father, too, will drive them away, to whatever destination they can manage.

Many a young beaver explores upstream or down, seeking uncontested territory where a new dam might be built and a new pond limit access to a new beaver lodge. This enterprise goes faster if the young beaver finds a mate and the two work together. More risk enters if the disbarred beaver must climb a hill to reach the next watershed, where suitable sites may still exist on a different river system. Worst, of course, is for the young animal to fail repeatedly to discover a new home until a predator or accident ends its life. Where beavers are numerous, this often is the final step that keeps the population constant and prevents destruction of the habitat.

This pattern of population control occurs far more widely than is generally believed. Separation of young from parents sometimes postpones their reproduction until too late in the year, and they die without progeny. It allows the combined effects of adverse weather, predators, parasites (including diseases), and repeated rejection by older members of the species to prevent population growth. No comparable control affects humankind wherever food can be obtained from elsewhere and the water supply is adequate.

Spreading Herons

Just occasionally you learn of young that have found a home far from their parents and developed a new population where none had been before. During the late 1920s some buff-backed herons from western Africa and Portugal managed to fly across the southern Atlantic Ocean and discover a use for their routine way of life in northeastern South America. No doubt, earlier attempts had been made, but previously the would-be colonists found no habitat they could fit. The new contingent of buff-backed herons met with cattle on ranches that people had established. Associating with the steers and cows, the herons could catch grasshoppers and other insects stirred up by the big grazers. Cattle did not object when the white egrets (buffy on head and neck only at breeding season) perched on their backs, the better to see insect prey. The birds became known quite logically as "cattle egrets." Some of them flew lesser distances over water to a few islands of the West Indies and later to Florida. Feeding and nesting wherever convenient, their young spread northward near the Atlantic coast all the way to Canada. Their arrival was duly noted by birdwatchers as an interesting addition to the local fauna.

Nowhere, it seemed, did the cattle egrets usurp either food or nest sites from native birds. They simply found a vacant ecological niche and moved in.

The most peculiar feature of this recent history is that buff-backed herons in similar habitats on the great Indian subcontinent spread eastward in the same years; outliers colonized Australia and, still more recently, New Zealand.

Rampant Rodents

Perhaps a similar behavior is shown by lemmings in the far north as their populations increase and cause crowding. For untold years these little short-tailed, short-legged rodents have attracted human attention by deserting their lichen ranges and traveling downhill as though seeking other places to colonize. A lemming that encounters a river plunges in and tries to swim across. Arctic predators, whether foxes or snowy owls, become satiated with lemmings and cease to bother the multitudes in plain sight. In years of extraordinary lemming emigration, even caribou and reindeer have been known to snatch a lemming and eat it, forsaking temporarily their vegetarian ways.

Lesser rodents in more temperate climates tend to be less obvious. Yet native voles or meadow mice (*Microtus*) run rampant in some years, particularly on soils with a high content of sodium salt. These prolific creatures, found from Alaska and Labrador to Guatemala and the northern two-thirds of Eurasia, have been known to erupt suddenly and then have their hungry populations collapse. Feral house mice could reproduce as fast but seem to find excessive competition from wild white-footed mice, which hide by day and use their prominent eyes and big ears to avoid danger in twilight or after dark.

With litters of four to eleven, one after another, a pair of mice or of rats could theoretically have a thousand descendants in a single year. This calculation assumes that food and space are plentiful and no deaths are caused by disease, accident, or any bird or beast of prey.

Fish with Energy

As you might expect, fish in their watery environment deal differently with their young in reproduction. A salmon or a trout, full of energy upon arrival at a suitable shallow place, begins digging a nest in the bottom. The fish lifts pebbles in its mouth and fans away smaller particles by vigorous use of its fins, then moves aside (if a male) or discharges a few hundred eggs (if a female). The male takes the place of his mate and sprays a cloud of sperm cells to fertilize the eggs and start development on its way. One or both parents may remain close by to drive off anything that might disturb their babies-to-be. Fish of these particular kinds may not stay around until their young hatch out. But fish of other kinds actually wait and pick up their eggs or their young in their capacious mouths and abstain from food until the little fish hatch out and can go off on their own. A male seahorse actually has a brood pouch into which his mate lays her eggs. He serves as combined custodian and transport system until one by one the diminutive seahorses pop out through the small opening in the pouch. Relieved of his burden, he may go off in search of a meal or stay close to repel any other fish that might eat his newly independent young. Since all seahorses rely for food upon tiny living creatures in the nearby water, the young have no need to do more than practice living on the same kind of diet the adults suck into their small mouths.

Seahorse parents never go very far from the reef or shallows where they were "born" in this way. Salmon travel hundreds or thousands of miles from the open sea to the streams in which they were hatched out. Atlantic salmon on both sides of the ocean cease feeding as soon as they swim into their natal stream to find places to spawn, then let themselves down to the sea again for more food and full recovery, ready to repeat the process the following year. Pacific salmon have steeper rivers coming from high elevations in the mountain chain, with many a waterfall or a major stretch of rapids to be bypassed before reaching a place to spawn. The Pacific species all make the strenuous trip a single time and die without returning to the sea. Their young develop in fresh water and grow quite a lot before letting themselves downstream to finish developing in salt water. Since they make the trip only once, they cannot learn how to do it; guidance must be inborn. We cannot believe that their parents, as a final gesture, taught their young where to go to follow the correct tradition. The most we can assume is that young provided with numbered metal tags return to the same stream when mature because they remember the flavor of its water—something distinctive that cannot be overlooked or confused with river water entering the Pacific from any other river along the coast between Oregon and Alaska. That special flavor must be learned indelibly before a young salmon on either coast sets off into the broad ocean to feed and mature.

Atlantic eels possess still more incredible inner guidance, for all of them hatch from eggs left at the bottom of the Sargasso Sea some dozens of miles south of Bermuda. The hatchlings weigh less than an equal volume of water and drift upward to the surface. There they swim west without a compass and get caught in the great warm surface current known as the Gulf Stream. It carries the young eels north some distance from the east coast of America, until great numbers set off toward the continent. Males remain in the low-salinity

132

water of river mouths, while females swim against the current—clambering over dams and the sides of waterfalls—to upper reaches of the stream. Some even set off on rainy nights across fields to permanent ponds in which they can feed and mature. Within a few years, each surviving female is two feet long or more, shiny silvery in the water, and ready to make the reverse trip, across a wet field if necessary before swimming downstream to rejoin the males at the edge of the sea. Now comes the hard part: to swim through the open ocean south to the Sargasso Sea, to dive to its bottom, mate, lay fertile eggs, and renew the tradition. The parents die there without giving any instructions or protection to their young. But the hatchlings follow their inner guidance and repeat the process, even changing shape as they travel the route their parents before them took to populate the streams and ponds with eels. Whenever we meet an eel, we marvel that it travels without a guide or a map, just once in a lifetime but always along the same route.

10

The Language of Bees

Surely learning is based on memory, and memory depends on a brain big enough or complex enough to store information. Often we assume that learning is limited to animals with warm blood or to those with a backbone and a brain of respectable size (the vertebrates). We assume that insects, spiders, and smaller creatures with tiny brains follow only inherited rituals, without the ability to remember much or to change their behavior according to experience. Are they marvels of miniaturization, able to learn?

Mechanical actions are called upon to explain any behavior of insects that suggests a benefit from experience. Thus, an ant on its way home to its nest could daub a trail of dots of odorous secretion. These could inform other workers who venture there, either that this tree branch is unproductive or is the way to a bonanza. No memory or learning would then be involved.

When a field worker bee from a honeybee hive discovers rich nectar in a flower, she fills her crop and makes the trip home as fast as she can. She arrives at the productive flower by a zigzag route, but she flies straight home, making a "bee-line" for the hive. If you catch one honeybee after another and release each while you watch carefully the direction it takes, you may learn from a few bees where their hive is located. Once inside her hive, the worker bee shares her nectar with other workers and also performs a special dance that alerts other bees to the opportunity they might exploit. As Nobel prizewinner Karl von Frisch discovered, the dance in darkness on the vertical face of the comb inside the hive informs neighboring bees what direction to take and how far to fly to reach the prize. Until von Frisch's tests were repeated by many other scientists, always with the same results, few scientists were willing to credit these insects with such learning and meaningful communication.

A bumblebee that flies quickly on a collision course with the "slipper" part of a lady's-slipper flower to pop through a concealed slit and gain access to nectar and pollen inside is rarely credited with having learned this trick and performed it many times before. Inexperienced bumblebees fumble all over the flower and try to enter by its back doorways, not knowing that these are easy exits after plunging through the front. Indeed, most bees have to learn each year how best to get nectar and pollen from the different flowers they meet. "Best" is whatever takes least time and energy expended in travel to achieve maximum gain. Each kind of flower differs slightly from all others in the exact location of its rewarding nectar. Before old age and tattered wings end a honeybee's foraging forever, she has learned dozens of techniques for exploiting her habitat. Rarely can she survive to use these memories in a second year.

Equally important to a bee or wasp is the direction to fly in returning to its nest. As these insects gather food and store it for their young, they have extra reason for remembering where their storage center lies. The domesticated honeybee makes a fresh survey of its hive location each day. Beekeepers count on this when they transport at night by truck a number of hives to be set out close to an orchard. The bees are expected to learn their new location and some landmarks, then carry pollen from flower to flower and ensure a good crop. At dawn, the bees emerge and examine their surroundings, then take off to visit the orchard flowers. By dark that evening, all of these insects will be back inside their hive, perhaps to be transported a hundred miles or more and to repeat the process in a different orchard the following day.

Technically, these flying insects are not babies anymore. Their early lives are spent as grubs within the confines of a hive, usually within individual brood chambers. Each grub has little opportunity to show what it might learn, for all its needs are attended to either in the form of food left beside it in its chamber or as fresh nourishment brought by an adult of its kind and regurgitated on a regular schedule. The first task the youngster may need to attempt is to seal up its cell when it is fully grown, ready to metamorphose during a fasting stage into the proper form of the adult insect. Breaking through its doorway to the outside world will be the next move made by the young adult.

A bumblebee, to take another example, hatches out within the confines of a cup-shaped chamber built by the queen herself with thin walls of wax. Close by she has another waxen cup filled with nectar that is gradually changing to honey. She rests atop her brood chamber where she can reach into the honeypot for nourishment. In her covering of stiff bristles, black and gold, she retains body heat which can be shared with the egg and later the hatchling, helping them develop more rapidly. After her egg hatches, she turns end-to-end many times each day and offers her grub regurgitated food. The grub accepts food whenever it is presented but shows no indication of begging for it or of interacting with its mother before or after a meal. At least once a week, the grub takes out time to shed its outer skin and expose a new one of slightly larger size. In a few weeks, the grub uses wax from its own glands to seal off its chamber, then proceeds to molt once more, exposing the different covering of the pupal stage. Now the outlines of antennae, legs, wings, and final body segments can be recognized. In warm weather, the pupa develops rapidly within its shell and gets ready to emerge as an adult bumblebee. Its actions will be totally different, with no need to remember anything from its development stages.

In summer, the mature bumblebee that emerges is equally likely to be an active male or a comparatively small female—a queen barely larger than he is. In autumn, most of the adults emerge as giant queens capable of foraging long after the first frost and gathering an inner store of food to last them until spring. They alone survive cold weather, to get busy feeding again and building nests early the following year. Often you see them on cold spring days, hunting for a disused chipmunk burrow, in the mouth of which the nest will have some protection, or visiting flowers for nectar before any other bees are active. It makes no difference that the chipmunk is still asleep in a deeper chamber, waking only occasionally to nibble at food it has stored under its grassy mattress or in adjacent rooms. The bumblebee is the one that experiences the cold weather and really makes use of its furlike coat.

The flight song of the bumblebee as it explores the flowers or searches for a nest site is one of the sounds we learn to recognize as children. Only by reminding ourselves of the differences in dimension between their lives and ours can we appreciate fully their reliance on seasonal displays of coded calls. How else could a small animal efficiently stake out a claim to a disused hole, a bush, or a clump of grass and with the same gesture invite an unseen mate to approach? Usually the insect has no time to waste because a single season encompasses its entire period of maturity. A week or two (or perhaps a month) affords all the chances to reproduce it will ever have. Any individual reaching adulthood too early or late is almost certain to leave no offspring.

Deciding when an insect, a spider, or a crab is "young" can be more challenging than to apply this description to vertebrates. Each of these invertebrates emerges from an egg with a body still lacking some of the features of its parents. After feeding and getting heavier, the creature splits its skin and reveals a new covering underneath—a fresh skin that will harden in a somewhat larger size, allowing obvious growth. Even most of the lining of the digestive tract is shed and replaced. Sometimes a change of diet is necessary, following inherited preferences. The individual may have to learn all over how best to behave, again with inherited guidance. We regard it as beginning its learning experience, like a human baby right after birth in its new environment.

11

Through Young Human Senses

Human babies are much like their parents. Although smaller and of slightly different shape, they could never be mistaken for the young of any other creature. With food, protection, and teaching they grow to maturity in less than two decades and claim as theirs a share of the adult world.

The age of a human individual may not be obvious from a photograph. Our best cues come from the proportions of the head and body. At birth the infant's head is already large, and it continues to grow rapidly, providing space for the brain. Before birth the human brain attains a fourth of its adult weight. By age six months it is half its final weight, and by a child's ninth birthday, it is almost full size. The youngster needs all the brain possible and the longest possible association with one or both parents, because it has to learn more than any other creature merely to survive in the human environment. We must rely upon our own special heritage—our unique cerebral cortex and our relatively unspecialized bodies—to benefit from personal experience begun at birth, as well as from the accumulated lore of civilization, and still further from what we can learn of the sensory riches of all other living animals. By expanding our avenues of awareness we stand to gain these benefits, fortifying our faith in the future.

So much do we rely upon a large rounded head and remarkably large eyes to reveal an individual's lovable infancy that we choose our pets with the same criteria in mind. Large-eyed, short-nosed animals release parental behavior within us, causing us to favor cats, terriers, pandas, bushbabies, and owls. Lower in interest are small-eyed, long-nosed creatures, such as rats, weasels, foxes, and opossums. Babies prefer a rounded face rather than an angular one. As though to benefit from this rule from infancy on, the pupils of human eyes open automatically as much as 17 percent in diameter when seeing something with appeal and close down a little when repelled. For a woman, a picture of a mother and baby has greatest effect—more than of the baby alone. Men respond little to photographs of babies or of mothers with infants but show a strong interest in landscape pictures—subjects toward which most women display a negative reaction. As might be expected, photographs of nude members of the opposite sex cause a prompt widening of the pupils, whereas those of members of the same sex do not elicit interest.

Among our most fascinating opportunities is to watch a human newborn explore its environment. Like us, it will soon forget how satisfying was its early discovery that its left hand could be held by its right. Those toes are the ends of its own feet and hurt if squeezed. That belly button is a place in which to hook a fingertip. Long before our second birthday, we can show an inexperienced baby-sitter how to position a diaper correctly and make its top secure. We learn that unpleasant events may follow if we throw things on the floor and that feigned innocence can be believed.

Wide-eyed ignorance of whatever happens becomes second nature. Someone else will take the blame and clean up, too. Parents unwittingly encourage us to develop this defense. They are the slow learners, as they adjust to having a smart baby in their midst. They cannot believe an infant could learn so quickly to influence them in its world.

Entranced, they watch our little fingers explore everything in reach. Objects small enough to pop into a baby's mouth have to be kept away for fear they might be swallowed. Bigger things still have a flavor when they reach our lips. We learn to spit out many that displease us. A short nose samples odors that longer adult noses fail to detect. At first we do not look at whatever makes a sound, but our ears record it all. Nobody recognizes that likes and dislikes are being associated, to guide us after we grow older and supposedly wiser. Carrots may seem yucky for years simply because Mother frowned over something else when she gave us our initial sample.

Toddlers are too young to tell in words what they feel. Instead they use facial expressions, body movements, and behaviors. All of these tell a lot, if we pay attention to them. Just by clinging to a skirt or trouser leg, the child shows difficulty in becoming independent and a need to be sure of parental love—that the care-giver will be there when needed. The arrival of a baby-sitter, a move to a different house, or any other rearrangement of the infant's world may instigate a regressive step, showing a wish to have things the way they used to be. Partial insights as to how the world works may confuse and frighten the child, bringing on a sudden episode of screaming and crying. Even inability to please the parent can frustrate and anger an infant, setting off a temper tantrum. Perhaps the child reduces those inner tensions merely by sitting on the floor and rocking back and forth or banging against the wall or the sides of the crib. A thumb to suck is comforting as it was before birth, more available than a nipple with milk, satisfying and reliable even if the parent tries to discourage the practice for fear that pressures inside the gum line will cause teeth to grow in crooked. What the infant really craves is to be sure that the same person will be there for support. It seeks limitless love and comfort. No overdose of either can do harm.

Often the parent or teacher measures progress on a comparative scale. Can the infant use its arms to raise up its chest at two months? Sit with support at four months? Sit alone at seven months? Creep at ten? Pull up to a standing position by twelve months? Climb steps at thirteen? Stand alone at fourteen? Walk alone at fifteen months?

Did babbling change to simple words at twelve to fifteen months? Mere understanding of "No!" doesn't count, for this comprehension precedes speech, beginning at eight to nine months with no ability of the infant itself to say "No!" until three to six months later. Vocabulary builds from three to fifty words during the first half of the second year. Two-word phrases and short sentences become common in the two-year-old. Memory helps the child to think before it acts and to recognize likely consequences. Now it may notice that one toy is missing and start a search for that particular item. Still more revolutionary is the change late in the second year, from self-centered speech to a burst of vocabulary and a new interest in the rest of the world. The child's own actions have become separated from those of others.

Almost incredibly, the unborn fetus is already alert to sounds it hears repeatedly. It learns distinctive features of its mother's voice and will show later by differences in sucking that a story read aloud to it several times before birth is better than something new. A man's voice is less familiar than any woman's and may cause a slight rise in the rate of fetal heartbeat, whereas the mother's voice slows the rate as though reassuring.

Acoustic cues—vowel and consonant changes—are recognized by six-month-olds regardless of voice pitch. "Computers that are supposed to do everything can't be programmed for every voice, but babies perform brilliantly," according to Patricia Kohl of the University of Washington. Research suggests that the child is not born as a blank slate and does not learn to speak by parroting. Peter Jusczyk, a psychologist at the University of Oregon, found that at about ten months, babies begin registering the particulars of their own language but that infants have the capacity to be multilingual. At four days they discriminate between such closely related sounds as *ba* and *pa*. It also appears that they can tell languages apart: In measuring the baby's sucking pattern, changes occur in eye movements as they respond to projected images of a woman reading in two different languages. Babies' sensitivity to speech begins even before birth. In utero, Jusczyk says, they hear "the melody of language. It probably sounds like people talking through the walls of a motel room." This sensitivity shows after birth as clues to which sounds go together. French scientists tested the idea that speech awareness begins before birth by inserting a tiny audio device in the birth canal. Then, expectant mothers were asked to read aloud one of two stories, several times a day during the last weeks of pregnancy. Three days after birth, the infants listened to recordings with padded earphones. By monitoring sucking patterns, it was found that the babies showed a preference for the sounds of stories they had been read to in utero. But there is no evidence that talking to a child in the womb makes it smarter. It is the give-and-take with adults and older siblings that appears to have a bearing on an infant's language development. Anthony DeCasper says, "Language doesn't spring full blown from a child's head like magic, there are very small steps kids take linked to learning from caretakers." And linguistic revolutionary Noam Chomsky indicates that the environment is no more than a triggering mechanism for language, in the same way that nutrition triggers growth.

Following its birth, a baby learns quickly that its primary need for food is reduced less by squirming and crying than by gaining access to its mother. Its physiological needs recede, and safety needs take their place. Needs for love and belonging come by the end of a human infant's first year, then by age three years, greater needs for self-esteem through social approval by parents and peers. Early years at school show a growing need for competency and acceptance. First-graders long for evidence that they are valued. They will work hard at tasks that as yet make no sense to them, merely to receive praise from the teacher or to escape failing with peers as witnesses. A model to imitate, such as a same-sexed, similar-looking parent, offers special rewards. The sound of the voice or various acts may be copied rather than the complex person. "Don't!" is learned through identification with a warm, loving, powerful model who frequently says "don't!"

Little disappointments can have lasting effects. Disapproval of the taste of orange juice and a lifelong disdain for orange sherbet may follow one experience of total bafflement in childhood. For example, the dish of ice cream promised as a reward for cooperation in the hospital before having tonsils removed may have turned out to be orange sherbet. Seldom do we remember how these associations began or appreciate how long they last.

Some of a baby's preferences may be inherited. Having its right-handed mother carry the child on her left arm with its right around her neck and left hand free makes it skilled with both hands—not choosing to reach with just the left. However they are carried, more than eighty in each hundred babies will be right-handed anyway, fewer than ten will be left-handed, and the few others reasonably ambidextrous. Chemists recognize amino-acid chains as coming in left-handed and right-handed forms, with left the commoner type. This seems not to influence most snail shells, which coil to the right, or most galaxies of stars, which coil to the left. Parrots show an almost unbreakable choice of the left foot for manipulating foods while standing on the right. Dogs and cats are more ambidextrous. Cultural custom worldwide agrees that the hands on a clock should go to the right (clockwise, not counterclockwise) for those who have not transferred to a digital readout. Almost as uniform is that highway traffic should keep to the right and go around each circle counterclockwise. If you proceed counter to the majority of customers in a supermarket, you may start among the fresh vegetables and end up at the frozen-food display, just as you planned. The ice cream may stay hard until you get home, but the baby in the carrier will not know the difference. An awareness of handedness in people and pets comes high in the ladder of maturational changes.

Avenues of awareness differ in significance between human and nonhuman infants. A mother hen will hurry to rescue from a thin-walled cloth cage a chick she can hear peeping but not see. Yet the same mother will ignore her chick if it is confined in a class enclosure with soundproof walls. The chick can see her through the glass, and she must see the chick, for she will try to get through the glass if grain is sprinkled at the chick's feet. But her reactions then are solely to the food—something that appeals through her visual centers. Hearing is the only avenue to her protective instinct.

Jerome Kagan at Harvard University recognizes in infants a mix of temperamental qualities he regards as inborn. Only ten to fifteen in a hundred children begin with an outgoing personality, inviting parents and other care-givers to interact. An equal minority prove to be shy, cautious, and vigilant, postponing personal exploration while watching others for the effects of actions. These differences correspond to unlike rates of heartbeat and levels of hormones in the blood. Yet follow-ups reveal that these particular differences are unrelated to timidity or boldness in development, the child's growing sense of self-awareness, intelligence in later life, or other qualities of a human individual.

Most important among the inborn features in a human baby seems to be a readiness to learn and then to imitate. Reinforced by approval, imitation leads to language. Long before the child can talk, it is associating sequences of sound with events in its world. When it learns to say "red" or "green," it discovers that each refers to something special—a whole category of appearances. When the wrong word is used, someone corrects it, substituting the other. Gradually, the whole spectrum becomes known—the colors in a rainbow—always in the same sequence: red, orange, yellow, green, blue, violet. Black, gray, and white are something else, distinguishing dark and bright.

The baby's ears detect fainter sounds, and a greater range between low notes and high, than those of its parents. Already its sensitivity is being curtailed by changes that progress with age. Taste, too, identifies sweet and sour, bitter and salty, at concentrations much less than an adult needs to produce a clear sensation. The infant even has some taste buds on the roof of its mouth, which disappear by adolescence. The child is capable of more than it can describe but loses its borderline abilities before it can be puzzled by them in comparisons with its parents.

Even a child's mode of perceiving undergoes development before puberty. If preference is for relying on vision to decide what is vertical and what horizontal, cues may be ignored from inner ears and sense organs in skin, muscles, and tendons. These children usually show a youthful dependence upon companions and choose tasks they can perform in groups. Frequently they grew up in homes where parents were reluctant to delegate responsibilities or severely restricted youthful activities.

By contrast, youngsters who are willing to discredit vision if it conflicts with sensory cues to position in relation to gravity tend to be independent by nature, often becoming nonconformists. Generally they escaped early from parental ties and broadened their own interests as though trying to contend effectively with more features in the environment. Commonly they score higher on IQ tests because of greater skill in separating simple patterns from confusing complexity. They excel at using their senses in penetrating camouflage, although they seldom show special advantages in vocabulary, information, or comprehension. It is simply that, in everything they do or the way they do it, the eye-independent people show a greater readiness to decide "which way is up." Somehow our capacity for hanging a picture straight is linked to our ability to see a motionless bird in a bush. The sensations we gain are not determined solely by the things sensed or by the limitations of our sense organs. Our brain, too, makes its contribution, and therein lies much of the uniqueness in each person's interpretation of the universe.

Comparison between what mature people know and what a young one accepts brings out the areas of special learning. With less on its mind, a child may develop a deeper grasp of differences between athletic teams and follow the sports news with extra avidity. Few parents succeed in getting their youngsters to follow the stock market and recognize opportunities in playing it.

Until a child has traveled to a foreign land, exchange between currencies remains a mystery. Focusing on differences in religious beliefs and languages awaits travel experiences, too. So does an appreciation for unlike life forms: great apes, giraffes, zebras, and ostriches in Africa; goldenrods, hummingbirds, and wood warblers in the Americas; emus, marsupials, and egg-laying mammals in Australia; real oddities, perhaps of giant size, on remote islands. Common denominators, whether native or introduced, soon become familiar on any continent: cattle, deer, goats, rabbits, mice, cats, dogs and other canines, doves, sparrows, ducks, geese, hawks, owls, ants, bees, wasps, dragonflies, ladybugs, and a host of other insects.

We scarcely recognize how limited in the animal kingdom are creatures in which parents interact with their young and young with parents. Almost half the animal world follows developmental patterns that call for releasing reproductive cells into the sea or fresh waters and leaving them on their own to find one another, to catch food, and to grow and mature toward a day when they can shift to the same types of living spaces their parents occupied, there to repeat the process. The minority in the animal kingdom offers a bit more protection for the young, either by associating with a parent that fends off danger or by learning quickly from a parent how to survive in a hostile world. Because our human species follows this protected pattern, we think of it as the best during a baby's search for independence.

If we consider the various lifestyles and modes of learning to cope with the environment shown by nonhuman animals, we realize that these differences were bought by successes through an immensity of time. As a wise old naturalist used to tell us, "An animal generally gets along in whatever simple way its body will allow." Different bodies require different ways. Different bodies take unlike times to develop. Where development is fast and brief, the individual has no time to learn how to behave and, to survive, must inherit suitable guidance. Our own development takes so long to reach a reproductive age that the human mind can afford to start at

Young tigers are grouped with those of the animal babies that gain protection from their parents by association and by learning quickly to survive. Unlike plant eaters, young predators take longer to develop to subdue active prey. (Courtesy of V. Q. Taylor, Hampton, New Hampshire)

birth to learn what must be done. We have time to fumble and recover, to give each brain and memory a fresh start, so long as the personal experience adds no handicap.

As the most helpless at birth and the fastest to learn, the human baby contrasts completely with the world it inhabits. Our neighbors' children manage to survive and multiply while going through most of the same stages of development that we recognize in our own. Swiss psychologist Jean Piaget identified eight ladderlike stages in development, with no skipping allowed. A child at stage two can do things that were impossible at stage one but cannot yet accomplish tasks performed by a child at stage three. The first stage is infancy, when hope emerges and trust finds honest rewards. This works both ways: The baby learns to smile at a recognized caretaker, and the nurturing individual develops a loving sense of being needed. Second, in early childhood, comes a stubborn struggle for self-direction, a resolution of doubts, and feelings of shame. Self-awareness lets the child recognize its image in a mirror and notice that a strange child is harmlessly "like me," whereas an unfamiliar adult might be feared. Peer relationships, perhaps in a daycare center, have a separate significance, unlike interactions between children and adults. Third is a preschool age of play, when small failures engender a sense of guilt, and purpose gets recognition. Fourth is the school age, when industry produces competence and dispels inferiority. Fifth comes adolescence as the end of childhood, with its struggle for identity and overriding of confusion. Who am I, and what will be my occupation in life, become important questions. Satisfaction comes from meeting challenges that fit developing skills and provide meaningful rewards. Sixth is young adulthood, avoiding isolation and letting love come of age. Seventh is generative maturity, when individuals become parents and helping others becomes more of an achievable goal. Eighth and last is old age, appreciating wisdom while rejecting despair and adjusting to a slower pace. Each stage grades into the next, building on what went before and preparing for what is to follow. Or development may follow a more flexible schedule, affected both by age and the quality of the environment. To the degree that the individual has no need ever to stop learning, childhood continues throughout human and nonhuman life.

Recent changes in countries that are technologically advanced often alter the pattern in human lifestyle. No longer may the mother provide most of the nurturing because the husband is out of the house on weekdays during hours when the young child is awake. In one family where the roles abruptly reversed—the mother away at her job all day while the father tends the house and child—she tells us her four-year-old has switched to calling her Daddy when she arrives, insisting that the father who stays home is Mama!

Seldom does confusion in its world show so clearly. The child manages to sort things out with a minimum of guidance, often in details that the parent fails to recognize as potential problems. Failure to retrieve the correct word to communicate an idea provides only a momentary setback, from which progress with rewarding approval continues in other directions.

The stage at which a wild animal or human one is born and the particular pattern of growth it follows are clearly related to the environment from which its nourishment must come. The mother must have adequate food while she nurses her young, and the young must mature into a world where they can find their own food. Among the native animals of American fields and forest, we can find many that are more fully formed at birth than any pouched mammal but just as blind, deaf, hairless, and helpless as a newborn mouse or rat. Young groundhogs, each about four inches long, are like this when they are born, about a month after their mother has awakened from her winter sleep. Yet within three weeks they have fur, and the two to eight of them in a litter begin to crawl about in the burrow. A week later their mother brings them some plant food. At six weeks the youngsters are weaned and very playful. They still have most of the summer ahead of them, in which to eat and grow and mature.

Newborn chipmunks go through the same stages. At birth, the four or five of them born together in an underground chamber weigh less than a half ounce all together. A week later, they are four times as heavy; at two weeks of age, six times their birth weight; at three weeks, eight times; at four weeks, almost ten times. They stay with their mother until they are about three and a half months old. By then they are following her along stone walls and across woodland paths where they are easy to see. In their habits, their markings, and their body form they are definitely chipmunks. Yet when first born, almost no feature showed what they could grow up to be.

Like ourselves, by the time they are born, all other animals are as well along in the life patterns that are characteristic of their species as they need to be. And they cannot vary their basic inheritance. A mouse can never keep on growing and become a rat or grow still more and become an elephant. But once the baby is born, the animal's new life is influenced by the environment in which it unfolds. The surroundings affect the way in which the wild or human baby will use the inherited guidance that it received from its two parents. Its further steps in growth include more than just becoming bigger and older. In adjusting to the environment, within the limits that are established by heredity, each baby becomes unique.

The primates have so protracted a childhood that even old males take a patriarchal interest in protecting the family group. Gorillas—which man meets on the ground, since they are too heavy to do much climbing—are noted for the risks they will run to make sure the mothers and babies remain unmolested. Man's own conviction that "home is his castle" no doubt stems from these humble roots.

In infant animals, including humans, Peter Marler of Rockefeller University concludes that "innate responsiveness may become heavily overlain and transformed by learning during the passage to adulthood. Yet in subtle ways, it must guide the young along certain developmental paths particular to its species without necessarily sacrificing the many advantages of behavioral plasticity."

Babies come into our world with a capacity for more than we are aware of. Surprisingly they can learn more abstract concepts and respond to certain sounds that parents are responsible for than we realized, according to recent findings of Elliott Blass of Johns Hopkins University. He began with "a conviction we all share that there are vital behavioral phenomena that are tied in with vital physiological systems and we don't know much about them." He started to investigate links between behavior and physiology by wondering how baby rats learn to find their mother's nipples and then on to the same in humans.

Newborn rats are blind and deaf, so how do they behave? Blass discovered that baby rats search for a familiar odor about their mother and in that way attach to the nipple. If the mother's nipple is washed, the rats do not attach. The rats learn the mother's odor when they are still in the womb. By experiments, Blass and his associates found that the newborn rats seek out an odor that they associate with a pleasurable sensation. Before the rats ever suckle, the rat mother spends a great time licking the anal-genital area of her young, thereby stimulating them and, at the same time, exposing them to her odor. Blass then stroked newborn rat pups in the presence of citral, a tasteless, lemon-scented compound, and they subsequently approached similarly scented nipples. The rats can only learn to like the scent of citral during the first eight days of life. After that the behavior is locked.

Rats retain what they learn in infancy, and it affects their behavior as adults. Rats exposed to citral in the womb or stimulated in the presence of citral as infants will as adults prefer mates so scented. An infant reared in a certain scent will prefer a partner with the same scent.

A study of human behavior showed that "what the mothers did prior to nursing and their behavior during nursing was the critical thing." Infants between two and forty-eight hours old were taught to anticipate a taste of sucrose. If a baby's forehead was stroked and then the baby was given sucrose,

155

the baby would turn its head in the direction in which the sucrose was delivered. "Even a two-hour-old baby is capable of extracting the predictive relationship between events that precede the presentation of sucrose and the presentation itself." There was a crying response when "a violation of the relationship" occurred.

Human babies can learn to anticipate sucrose in response to certain sounds—an auditory rather than a tactile stimulus. Four sounds were paired with the delivery of sucrose solution—a click sound made by a castanet, a *ting* made by a triangle, a *psst* sound, and a *shhh* sound. It was a complete surprise to find that the only sound the babies associated with sucrose was the click. The babies were made attentive with the click sound, were calmed by the *shhh*, and ignored the *psst* and triangle sounds by just continuing to do what they were doing. Blass did a sound spectrogram and found that the clicks, kisses, and clucks that parents make are similar to the sound of the castanet. When he consulted Arnold Gould of the Smithsonian Institution, Gould told him that all mammals click to their young, that clicking is the primary mode of communication between mammals and their infants. "If you're a mammal, you click," Gould told Blass. So parents know what they are doing when they click or *shhh* their babies. Blass comments, "What we are showing is that babies can extract relations between related events. It is the way babies start to build up their knowledge of the world."

Suggested Reading

Animal Intelligence: Insights into the Animal Mind, eds. R.J. Hodge and Larry Goldman. Washington, D.C.: Smithsonian Institution Press, 1986.

Ardrey, Robert. *The Territorial Imperative.* New York: Atheneum, 1966.

Augros, Robert and George Stoneiu. *The New Biology.* New Science Library, 1987.

Caras, Roger. *The Private Lives of Animals.* New York: Grosset & Dunlap, 1974.

Carrighar, Sally. *Wild Heritage.* Boston: Houghton Mifflin, 1965.

Carthy, J.D. *Animal Behavior.* Aldus Books, 1965.

The Darwin Reader, eds. Marston Bates and Philip S. Humphrey. New York: Scribner's, 1956.

Durrell, Gerald and Lee. *Ourselves and Other Animals.* New York: Pantheon, 1987.

SELECTED READING

Eibl-Eibesfeldt, Irenaus. *Ethology: The Biology of Behavior.* New York: Holt, Rinehart & Winston, 1970.

Fossey, Dian. *Gorillas in the Mist.* Boston: Houghton Mifflin, 1983.

Fox, Michael W. *Behavior of Wolves, Dogs and Related Canids.* Boston: Little, Brown, 1984.

Gibson, Janice T. *Growing Up.* Reading, Mass.: Addison-Wesley, 1978.

Gould, James L. *Ethology.* New York: Norton, 1982.

Gould, Stephen Jay. *Ontology and Phylogeny.* Cambridge: Belknap Press of Harvard University, 1977.

Marler, Peter, et al. *The Marvels of Animal Behavior.* Washington, D.C.: National Geographic Society, 1972.

Marler, Peter and William J. Hamilton, III. *Mechanisms of Animal Behavior.* New York: Wiley, 1967.

Milne, Lorus J. and Margery. *The Ages of Life.* New York: Harcourt, Brace & World, 1968.

————. *The How and Why of Growing.* New York: Atheneum, 1972.

————. *Patterns of Survival.* Englewood Cliffs, N.J.: Prentice-Hall, 1967.

————. *The Senses of Animals and Men.* New York: Atheneum, 1972.

————. *A Time to be Born.* San Francisco: Sierra Club Books, 1982.

Pringle, Lawrence. *Exploring the World of Wolves.* New York: Scribner's, 1983.

Social Behavior and Communication, eds. Peter Marler and J.C. Vandenbergh. New York: Plenum Press, 1979.

Tinbergen, Niko. *Social Behavior in Animals.* New York: Wiley, 1959.

Wickler, Wolfgang. *The Sexual Code.* Garden City, N.Y.: Doubleday, 1972.

Wilson, E.O. *Sociobiology.* Cambridge: Belknap Press of Harvard University, 1975.

Index